# Books by John Updike

## POEMS

*The Carpentered Hen* (1958) · *Telephone Poles* (1963) · *Midpoint* (1969) · *Tossing and Turning* (1977) · *Facing Nature* (1985) · *Collected Poems 1953–1993* (1993) · *Americana* (2001) · *Endpoint* (2009)

## NOVELS

*The Poorhouse Fair* (1959) · *Rabbit, Run* (1960) · *The Centaur* (1963) · *Of the Farm* (1965) · *Couples* (1968) · *Rabbit Redux* (1971) · *A Month of Sundays* (1975) · *Marry Me* (1976) · *The Coup* (1978) · *Rabbit Is Rich* (1981) · *The Witches of Eastwick* (1984) · *Roger's Version* (1986) · *S.* (1988) · *Rabbit at Rest* (1990) · *Memories of the Ford Administration* (1992) · *Brazil* (1994) · *In the Beauty of the Lilies* (1996) · *Toward the End of Time* (1997) · *Gertrude and Claudius* (2000) · *Seek My Face* (2002) · *Villages* (2004) · *Terrorist* (2006) · *The Widows of Eastwick* (2008)

## SHORT STORIES

*The Same Door* (1959) · *Pigeon Feathers* (1962) · *Olinger Stories* (a selection, 1964) · *The Music School* (1966) · *Bech: A Book* (1970) · *Museums and Women* (1972) · *Problems* (1979) · *Too Far to Go* (a selection, 1979) · *Bech Is Back* (1982) · *Trust Me* (1987) · *The Afterlife* (1994) · *Bech at Bay* (1998) · *Licks of Love* (2000) · *The Complete Henry Bech* (2001) · *The Early Stories: 1953–1975* (2003) · *My Father's Tears* (2009) · *The Maples Stories* (2009)

## ESSAYS AND CRITICISM

*Assorted Prose* (1965) · *Picked-Up Pieces* (1975) · *Hugging the Shore* (1983) · *Just Looking* (1989) · *Odd Jobs* (1991) · *Golf Dreams* (1996) · *More Matter* (1999) · *Still Looking* (2005) · *Due Considerations* (2007) · *Hub Fans Bid Kid Adieu* (2010) · *Higher Gossip* (2011) · *Always Looking* (2012)

## PLAY

*Buchanan Dying* (1974)

## MEMOIRS

*Self-Consciousness* (1989)

## CHILDREN'S BOOKS

*The Magic Flute* (1962) · *The Ring* (1964) · *A Child's Calendar* (1965) · *Bottom's Dream* (1969) · *A Helpful Alphabet of Friendly Objects* (1996)

# BUCHANAN DYING

# John Updike

# BUCHANAN DYING

## A PLAY

Random House Trade Paperbacks • *New York*

2013 Random House Trade Paperback Edition

Copyright © 1974 by John Updike
Foreword copyright © 2000 by John Updike

Published in the United States by Random House Trade Paperbacks,
an imprint of The Random House Publishing Group,
a division of Random House, Inc., New York.

RANDOM HOUSE TRADE PAPERBACKS and colophon are trademarks
of Random House, Inc.

Originally published in the United States in hardcover by Alfred A.
Knopf, a division of Random House, Inc., in 1974. The foreword was
originally published by Stackpole Books, Mechanicsburg, Pa., in 2000.

ISBN 978-0-8129-8490-3
eBook ISBN 978-0-307-96186-0

Printed in the United States of America

www.atrandom.com

2 4 6 8 9 7 5 3 1

# *Foreword to the Stackpole Books Edition*

The original edition of *Buchanan Dying*, in 1974, carried as preface this brief "Note":

> Even the writer of a closet drama imagines himself the first and lowliest laborer at a glittering edifice of collaboration. Were this play to be produced, care should be taken with the lighting and the accents. The one-room set should be simple but solid; darkness will transform it into a forest, a cabin, or an inner arena. A few changes of furniture make Wheatland the White House. Spotlighting must be used to permit actors to withdraw, where exits are not specified. Contrariwise, when the political speeches are given, the entire audience might be illuminated, as part of the scene. As to the accents: the utterances that have descended to us in historical records and memoirs, which I have tried to blend with utterances imagined, are couched in the rounded and scarcely idiomatic public language of the nineteenth century. But the geographical breadth of this cast of characters, and the conflicts among them, can live in their accents; the Southern accent, especially, must be heard by the audience, as it was by Buchanan, as an insistent, melodious tugging.

These blithe and grandly simple directives were put to the test in two subsequent productions. First, the play was performed, with all the trimmings of costume and stagecraft, at

Franklin and Marshall College in Buchanan's own town of
Lancaster, Pennsylvania, from April 29th to May 8th, 1976,
in the Green Room Theatre. Edward S. Brubaker directed
the production and cut the text to bring it within a playable
time. Peter Vogt played the protagonist, Leslie Stainton (who
has recently come forth with a biography of the Spanish poet
Lorca) was Harriet Lane, and Shevaun Keogh took the allur-
ing triple role of Anne Coleman, Susan Sparks Keitt, and the
Czarina of Russia, in which latter persona she displayed a
dazzling French accent and a wealth of glittering jewels. The
next year, in March of 1977, six performances were mounted
by the Institute for Readers Theatre at San Diego State University, thanks in large part to the personal enthusiasm and
energy of Robert McCoy, an associate professor of English
there. McCoy directed, and the demanding part of Buchanan
was enacted by Sheldon Gero; Pam Adams played Harriet
Lane and Lenetta Kidd performed as Anne Coleman and her
avatars. The full text was also shortened for this production,
in which the uncostumed actors read—with animation, of
course—from unmemorized scripts.

Both brave, dutiful versions have faded in my mind, these
twenty-some years later, but for a few details such as Miss
Keogh's fine accent and Mr. Gero's evident restless agony as
he lay immobilized within Buchanan's long and wordy dying.
It is a cruel play to inflict on a performing company, it occurred to me as I sat in the audience. No further productions
have been proposed. (One nibble from public television came
with the sharp hook that it all would have to be revised, along
sensible lines proposed by sensibilities other than the author's.) As I watched, on these two occasions, brightly lit stage
actors moving through my basically verbal and inward drama,
I wondered if a motion picture, with its fluid scene-shifts and

facial closeups, was not what I had written. Playwrights tell of
their rapture in seeing their words recited on the stage; my
own sensations were discomfiture and pity for these pretty
flies I had trapped in my dreamy amber. Trying to remember
the play in performance, I come up with backstage irrelevan-
cies: my mother attended the Lancaster performance and
looked regal—every inch a first-nighter—wearing a gray fox
fur I had given her from a trip to Russia twelve years before,
and my wife-to-be went with me to San Diego, which we had
expected to be summery in March and where we nearly froze
in our thin clothes as we hurried across the great paved spaces
of the campus. Both female companions, needless to say, were
loyal to the playwright and his play, but I could not help sus-
pecting that the event they graced had been at bottom disap-
pointing: a full-length portrait of political impotence and
private timidity may be better suited to a book read in solitude than to the social festivity of the theatre, with its ancient
roots in proclamatory rite and religion.

Yet the book itself, falling so curiously between several
stools, was lightly reviewed—at most thoughtful length by
the historian Arthur Schlesinger, Jr., in *The Atlantic Monthly*,
and not at all in *The New York Times*, which has a policy against
reviewing published plays—and sold proportionately, though
it did creep into a small second edition. Over the years Alfred
A. Knopf, Inc., allowed its handsomely designed and typeset
volume to drift out of print. Now we have this new printing
by Stackpole Books, which differs from the Knopf text only
by a score of small corrections and the addition of this foreword. I had long harbored a hope of revising the play, cutting
it down to two practicable, symmetrical, rather Beckettian
acts—first, Buchanan, yielding to blandishments to be more
dynamic, slowly gets out of bed; second, Buchanan is beaten

back to bed, where he completes his dying. Two rereadings
persuaded me that less might be, after all, merely less. Will-
fully wandering as the drama is, it does hold most of what I
wanted to say about the fifteenth President, in his long and
various career. Exhaustiveness is a novelist's method, and
what we have here is a kind of novel, conceived in the form of
a play, with an ample afterword composed of leftovers.

Readers now might have to be reminded, as readers in 1974
did not, of the national protest over Vietnam, which at its
height prevented President Johnson from publicly speaking
in any venue less sheltered than a television studio or a military installation. Had any President been so vilified—the play
*MacBird* marking a low point in the slander and venom—
since Buchanan himself? A President, unlike the leader of a
parliamentary system, cannot ask for a vote of confidence and
resign if none forthcomes; he is stuck with his elected term
and his chosen policies, even when strident popular opposition arises. The questions raised in the crisis years 1965–1973
find echo in the pre–Civil War crisis, when a peaceable, com-
promising, legalistic President presided over a widening split
no compromise or legalisms could bridge. Harriet Lane,
faced with the indignant grief of an old friend turned war
protester, asks, "Does power only contaminate? If public office become perforce vile, then none but villains will choose
to serve." Buchanan puts it, "Society for its manifold blessings asks in exchange sacrifice and compromise. Concession
is the world's walking gait. . . . Government is either organized benevolence or organized madness; its peculiar magnitude permits no shadings." He himself is something of a
peacenik, dreading the men of violent action of whom Andrew Jackson is his chief exemplar; the Reverend Paxton tells

him, "In truth you disdain these heroes as brutes of delusion and spendthrifts of blood." And the dying Buchanan cringes from the smell of blood emanating from the apparition of Lincoln.

Leadership of any country but one in a comic operetta involves some decisions whose consequences are bloody. The problem is not as simple as the chant, "Hey, hey, LBJ, How many kids did you kill today?" By pursuing a tactical conflict on the other side of the world, LBJ, rightly or wrongly, thought he was saving kids from worse nearer wars. True, he had a streak of the bully and did escalate a war, whereas Buchanan evaded beginning one, leaving his successor an unlit powderkeg. Still, my attempt was to extend sympathy to politicians, as they make their way among imperfect alternatives toward a hidden future. To phrase this sympathy in terms of the overheated years leading up to the Civil War, deploying much mid-nineteenth-century rhetoric and some generally forgotten political issues of the time, was to ask a good deal of my audience. We can absorb historical details as they foreshadow a national icon's triumph, as in such plays as *Sunrise at Campobello* and *Abe Lincoln in Illinois*. But when they are summoned to illuminate a figure as obscure, calumniated, and problematical as Buchanan, and used to illustrate my thesis that the pattern of his Presidency was established in an unfortunate broken romance of his young manhood, and to further propose that a dark thread in his life ran from his stern father through a number of personal and political enemies right up to God Himself—well, the attention of even an ideal audience, iron-bottomed and rabbit-eared, might be strained.

So with this newly reissued book in your hands you are in the best position to share my one excursion into American history. The stage, my original "Note" might have said, is your head; the actors and actresses and their costumes and gestures are yours for the conjuring. Cursory stage directions like (*gasps and hubbub*) might have been multiplied without easing the reader's task. I still suspect that my initial conception of a small novel, of four alliterative chapters, with dates running down the outside margin, was the correct one, had I had the wit and confidence to execute it.

I did return to the Buchanan matter in a 1992 novel, *Memories of the Ford Administration*, the purported narrative of a historian, Alfred L. Clayton, living in New Hampshire and working on a biography not, as you might suspect, of Franklin Pierce but of Pierce's successor, the fifteenth President. In scenes of historical fiction alternating with Clayton's memories from the frisky mid-seventies I drew closely upon some of the play's scenes—tea with the Hubley sisters, the walk with Andrew Jackson, the 1860 Cabinet meetings—and made up others, such as a diplomatic conversation with Hawthorne in England in 1855 and a kind of lovesong to fellow-Senator W. R. D. King in the form of a Congressional speech that Buchanan delivered early in 1838. By interposing a fallible narrator, who openly writes of the difficulties of achieving historical precision, and even accurate personal memory, I hoped to maneuver access to my elusive hero. But the effort to delve into history left me convinced of the unconscionable amount of bluff, fraud, and elision that any allegedly historical account, labeled fiction or not, entails. It is alarming to me that historical novelists openly brag that they have knowingly distorted the record, transposing dates and fudging conversations in the name of some supposed higher truth. But what truth can be higher than what actually did happen, moment by moment, incident by incident?

To be sure, total consecutive truth is lost, along with most of the artifacts of our daily life, all but a few of our spoken words, and all of our precious feelings. Time's grinding chews it all up. What remains even of twentieth-century events is an approximation and stylization, born of hasty records and rough-hewn news reports. Nevertheless, I felt that my sense of American reality was enhanced by my dip into nineteenth-century records and reports. To read of how the republic struggled to keep slavery even as that institution's barbarism became unignorable, and of how an elected government desperately sought the glue to hold opposed sections together under the sacred Constitution, and of how personal interchanges in Washington influenced and reflected vast and fatal issues, and of how private psychology was translated into national policy, and above all to read historians—to relax into the humane, tolerant, encompassing voice of an Allan Nevins or a Roy Nichols, and to marvel at how they shape a coherent story out of a million happenstances—all this benefited my ongoing education, adding a bit to my credentials as an American writer.

A writer educates himself in order to educate others, and the mixed, even jagged texture of this particular work testifies how far from smooth the transfer can be. But that some transfer takes place here, not just of information but of the affection behind my initial and enduring interest in the eminent Pennsylvanian James Buchanan, I dare to hope, and this new edition seems to confirm.

J. U.
*2000*

I wanted to write a novel in which the chief character was to have been a man who had a pair of spectacles with one lens that reduced as powerfully as oxy-gas-microscope and the other that magnified equally powerfully; in his interpretation everything was very relative.

—Søren Kierkegaard, in his *Journals*, December 10, 1837

I went into the Senate-chamber and heard a closing debate on Benton's Pre-emption bill. Sharp-shooting between Henry Clay and the sneaking scrivener, Buchanan.

—John Quincy Adams, in his *Diary*, January 20, 1841

Mr. Buchanan is an able man, but in small matters without judgement, and sometimes acts like an old maid.

—James K. Polk, in his *Diary*, February 22, 1848

The President divides his time between crying and praying; the Cabinet has resigned or else is occupied in committing treason. Some of them have done both. . . . Every one takes to politics for an occupation, but do you know to me this whole matter is beginning to get stale. It does not rise to the sublime at all. It is merely the last convulsion of the slave-power, and only makes me glad that the beast is so near his end. . . . In Massachusetts all are sound except Rice, but we've some pretty tight screws on him, and I think he'll hold. . . . But Pennsylvania is rotten to the core just as she was in the revolution when John Adams had such a battle with Dickinson. . . . Mr. Amory told us the other day of a letter he had seen from a New York stock merchant, which ran like this: "The market today much affected by political rumors of disturbing tendency. Toward the close of the day a report was circulated that President Buchanan had gone insane, and stocks rose." . . . Poor old Buchanan! I don't see but what he'll have to be impeached. The terror here among the inhabitants is something wonderful to witness.

—Henry Adams, in letters to his brother Charles,
December 18, 22, 26, 1861

But Mr. Buchanan was eminently a conscientious man. He had an oath registered on high to execute the laws, not to violate them. He was in his nature infinitely above that vulgar herd of perjured usurpers and cut-throats who have crimsoned the annals of the ages by their crimes, but to whom, alas, the world has bowed its neck and knee, and obsequiously erected its monuments.

—Joseph Holt, in a letter to James Buchanan Henry, May 26, 1884

# CAST OF CHARACTERS

(in order of appearance)

JAMES BUCHANAN, *statesman*, 1791–1868.

ESTHER PARKER ("Miss Hetty"), *housekeeper*, 1806–1899.

ANN COOK, *serving girl*, 18??–18??.

HARRIET LANE JOHNSTON, 1833–1903.

ROBERT COLEMAN, *ironmaster*, 1748–1825.

JOHN SLIDELL, *politician*, 1793–1871.

JOHN FORNEY, *journalist*, 1817–1888.

ELLIE REYNOLDS, 1835–1923.

LAWRENCE KEITT, *politician*, 1824–1864.

ANNE CAROLINE COLEMAN, 1796–1819.

GEORGE COLEMAN, *gentleman*, 1790–1821.

JASPER SLAYMAKER, *lawyer*, 1787–1827.

JOHN REYNOLDS, *editor*, 1787–1853.

MARIA BUCHANAN MAGAW JOHNSON YATES, 1795–1849.

EDWARD BUCHANAN, *clergyman*, 1811–1895.

MARY FIELD HUBLEY JENKINS, 1789–1867.

GRACE PARR HUBLEY, 1787–1861.

ELIZABETH SPEER BUCHANAN, 1767–1833.

ALEKSANDRA FEDOROVNA, *Empress of Russia*, 1798–1861.

ANDREW JACKSON, *statesman*, 1767–1845.

STEPHEN DOUGLAS, *politician*, 1813–1861.

JAMES POLK, *statesman*, 1795–1849.

HOWELL COBB, *politician*, 1815–1868.

MARY ANN LAMAR COBB, 1818–1889.

JOHN BUCHANAN FLOYD, *politician*, 1806–1863.

# CAST OF CHARACTERS

SALLY PRESTON FLOYD, 1802–1879.

SUSAN[NA] SPARKS KEITT, 1834–1915.

WILLIAM PORCHER MILES, 1822–1899. ⎫ *members of the*

JOHN MC QUEEN, 1804–1867. ⎪ *South Carolina*

MILLEDGE LUKE BONHAM, 1813–1890. ⎬ *congressional*

WILLIAM WATERS BOYCE, 1818–1890. ⎭ *delegation*

JEREMIAH BLACK, *lawyer*, 1810–1883.

JEFFERSON DAVIS, *statesman*, 1808–1889.

EDWIN STANTON, *politician*, 1814–1869.

JACOB THOMPSON, *politician*, 1810–1885.

ROBERT WOODWARD BARNWELL, 1801–1882. ⎫ *South Carolina*

JAMES LAWRENCE ORR, 1822–1873. ⎬ *"Commissioners"*

JAMES HOPKINS ADAMS, 1812–1861. ⎭

JOSEPH HOLT, *lawyer*, 1807–1894.

CHARLES SUMNER, *politician*, 1811–1874.

ABRAHAM LINCOLN, *statesman*, 1809–1865.

JAMES BUCHANAN, *tradesman*, 1761–1821.

WILLIAM PAXTON, *clergyman*, 1824–1904.

SAMUEL BLACK, *lawyer*, 1818–1862.

HIRAM SWARR, *executor*, 1821–1896.

# BUCHANAN DYING

# ACT I

*Wheatland, in Lancaster, Pennsylvania. May 31, 1868.* BU-
CHANAN, *a large old man with an upstanding crest of white hair,
lies in bed asleep, propped up on bolsters. The bed is not a four-poster
but a "sleigh bed," built of apple, cherry, and peach wood. Beyond
the bed a tall window with green Venetian blinds gives on darkness.
Beside the bed, a straight chair where visitors can sit, and a table
containing little—a pitcher, a glass, a mantle lamp, a well-worn
calfbound Bible. The correspondent for the New York* World *wrote
that "The room, which has always been his own favorite choice, is a
plain chamber . . . with . . . no other ornaments than two pieces of
old-fashioned embroidery, done by his mother when he was a child,
and marked in the corners, 'J. Buchanan.'" This is the so-called
Back Bedroom, preferred by the dying man perhaps because, being
over the kitchen, it was warm. Visitors enter stage left, having come
up a narrow winding stair. Servants may exit stage right, passing
through the mahogany-paneled bathroom, with its deep zinc-lined
tub that the master had built himself upon his return from the
White House. We do not see this bathroom but do see, unauthenti-*

*cally, stage left, on the same wall as the window, the iron-fronted fireplace that in fact is located catercornered across the room, and a bentwood rocker, and a low desk, and, above the fireplace mantel, the portrait of* ANNE COLEMAN *that truly hangs in the Master Bedroom.* MISS HETTY, *a plain woman past sixty, stands at the foot of the bed, dressed in gray, with an apron. A* NEGRO GIRL *in a canary-yellow dress waits motionless in a corner.*

BUCHANAN *struggles for breath, awakes, asks:* Miss Hetty?

MISS HETTY: I am here, Mr. Buchanan. Right here where you can see me.

BUCHANAN (*focusing*): Indeed you are. Indeed. What a mercy. I had a strange dream, Miss Hetty. A strangely substantial and distressing dream.

MISS HETTY: And what sort of dream might that have been, Mr. Buchanan?

BUCHANAN: I dreamed I was President of these United States.

MISS HETTY (*moving to bed, neatening up blankets, pillows*): But that's no more than fact.

BUCHANAN: None the less strange for that. Years ago, Miss Hetty, setting out to be a lawyer with old Jim Hopkins as my guide, I soon learned that facts are generally over-esteemed. For most practical purposes, a thing is what men think it is. When they judged the earth flat, it was flat. As long as men thought slavery tolerable, tolerable it was. We live down here among shadows, shadows among shadows.

MISS HETTY *folds down blankets, turns* BUCHANAN *over on his side, facing her and away from the audience. She places a bedpan below his middle. He emits a squeak of pain; then there is the sound of urination into the pan. She takes the bedpan away and hands it to the* SERVANT GIRL, *who carries it from the room.*

BUCHANAN: They were all there, Miss Hetty, as real to me as you are this minute—little Cobb fair to bursting to speak his piece, like the student certain to please the teacher, and Judge Black as dour and grim and rumpled in his clothes as a Glasgow chimney sweep, and old Cass struggling to stay awake with his wig slipping sideways, and poor John Floyd yellow as a ghost stretched out on the divan in his dressing gown, too sick with himself to stand; they all were wanting something from me, Miss Hetty. They were demanding I perform some task. I couldn't for the life of me make out what it was. They were frightened, Miss Hetty, every man of them. And I stood above them as majestic and serene as one of those pinioned eagles that used to roam the lawn.

MISS HETTY: Oh, weren't they fine pests! Killing the chickens, fouling the porch steps, keeping the dogs in a state of agitation . . . (*She accepts the emptied bedpan from the* SERVANT GIRL, *replaces it beneath the bed.*)

BUCHANAN: I was standing among them tall as a tree, Miss Hetty, exalted by the consciousness that I was President; my body felt to be composed of millions of spirits, and I flew, that's right, I was flying across the land, across the Alleghenies, and I thought to myself, Miss Hetty, I remember thinking, "I haven't been this far west since I rode to Kentucky at the age of twenty-one." I intended, you know, to go there and live. Had I done so, history would be different, and dear Anne might be alive. How strange facts are!

MISS HETTY: I always thought it strange, speaking of strange, how content those eagles acted on the lawn, considering they were native to California, where the scenery must be very different.

BUCHANAN: Ah, Lancaster County, its beauty becalms us all. Elsewhere in the United States men move on, but here they stick like flies to molasses paper. I take it, Miss Hetty, my dream has ceased to exercise a claim upon your interest.

MISS HETTY: Far from it, Mr. Buchanan. You were an eagle headed west.

BUCHANAN: I was the President, Miss Hetty, and all the Union lay visible beneath me. The North with its smoking mills, the soft green Southland as yet unscarred by war, the West with its deserts and mountains, the Mormon lake, the shining Pacific beyond. Beneath me lived a vast humming, which became a murmurous cry, a subdued and multitudinous petitioning for mercy; while above me a profound silence obtained, a silence as crystalline and absolute as a ladle of water from my corner spring. (*touches throat*) Tell me, could the child—might the child be prevailed upon to fetch a fresh pitcher from the spring? My system is so replete with poisons, none but the purest element can penetrate.

MISS HETTY *wordlessly hands* GIRL *the porcelain pitcher.* GIRL *goes out.*

BUCHANAN: Now tell me, dear all-knowing Hetty, what might my dream signify?

MISS HETTY: Maybe that you're remembering the old days in your sleep.

BUCHANAN: Come, Hetty. Humor an invalid. Play Joseph to my Pharaoh. What would the *hexerei* doctor behind Duke Street decipher of my flying?

MISS HETTY: Maybe that you're gaining back your strength.

BUCHANAN: No. Not that. We regain what is rightfully ours. I have exhausted my claim in this instance. Thrice, by my accounting, I was brought to the door of death and allowed to turn away. Once to become an officeseeker, when I would have joined poor deluded Anne in her grave. The second time, to become President, when my guts were all but dissolved with the National Hotel disease. The third time, to write my administration's vindication, though North and South were howling me down for a traitor and death had become as plentiful as apples in autumn. I seek no further reprieve. The carrying costs of my body have grown exorbitant. My effluviums, save for the giddy outpourings of speech, clog like a silted millrace, and the pain in my joints at night would make a Stoic seek his warm bath. My toes, for all the messages they send me, might be in session in Sacramento. Mix with these omens my curious bliss, my birthday sense of some wonder proximate, and the augury is firm. Flying equals dying. The oddity, dear Hetty, the philosophical oddity is that, having delayed dying so long, I find myself so skillful at it. I believe it has always been, unbeknownst, my *métier.* There is a saying of La Rochefoucauld's—"Peu de gens savent être vieux." Few men know how to be old. I am one of the few. Dying, I discover, is rather like dancing, and not unlike diplomacy; legerity and tact are paramount. I was a fair country dancer in my time.

MISS HETTY: Hush, Mr. Buchanan. For the sake of those that love you, hush. (*Bell rings downstairs.*) That must be Mr. Swarr. (*She leaves the room.* BUCHANAN, *alone, composes himself for prayer.*)

BUCHANAN: Dear Lord, without whose witness not the merest sparrow falls exhausted to the earth, make me worthy of my dying. Let me in this my last agony shed upon those around me comfort and reassurance of Thy merciful and omnipotent Providence. Let my example mollify for others Thy adamant will. Fill my failing heart with complacency of Heaven; then judge me truly, and cast me down with devils if I so deserve. Otherwise, enroll me in Thy chosen company eternally. Thy will be done, Amen.

*Footsteps have hastened the end of this prayer. The* BLACK CHILD *enters with the pitcher of spring water.*

BUCHANAN: Bless you, girl. Was it heavy for you?

GIRL: No, sah. I tote wood up to here sometimes. (*indicates top of head*)

BUCHANAN: What is your name, pray?

GIRL: They calls me Ann.

BUCHANAN: Not Ann Cook, surely?

GIRL: Yes, sah.

BUCHANAN: But I bought you out of slavery over thirty years ago; you and your mother Daphne. You were but five years old.

GIRL: Yes, sah.

BUCHANAN (*aside*): I've frightened her into imbecility.

GIRL: Here's de water, sah.

BUCHANAN: Could you—could I trouble you to fill a glass and hold it to my lips? My hands (*weakly lifts them, lets drop*), my hands have seceded. (*She pours.*) Thank you, my child. (*She holds glass to his lips; he drinks; the sound is amplified. He sinks back.*) Ah. Just reflect, if so much goodness resides in a simple element, how much richer and more propitious is the complex nature of a man! Do you understand me?

GIRL: No, sah.

BUCHANAN: Come a little closer, child. Look into my eyes. Is there anything strange about them?

GIRL (*looks, and arrives at judgment slowly*): Well, sah, one o' dem is blue, and de odder is more toward the color ob a frog half-hidin' hisself in de mud.

BUCHANAN: Exactly. Hazel, we call that color. And would you like to know a fact more curious still?

GIRL: Yes, sah.

BUCHANAN: The blue one is farsighted, and the other is near-sighted. When I close that one, you are blurred because you are too near, and when I close this one, you are blurred because you are too far away. But when I open them both, and tilt my head, you are in focus absolute, and I perceive even the tiny chocolate dimple (*with palsied effort he lifts his arm and touches her face*) there!

GIRL (*backs away, startled*): Yes, sah.

BUCHANAN: Seventy-seven this April last, and never needed spectacles. When they had me in the White House, I read dispatches past every midnight with no light greater than a candle betwixt my face and the page. Harriet and James Henry had the fear I would fall asleep and set myself afire, but I never did. I never did. I was tougher than they thought, the rascals, all the rascals north and south—tougher than they thought. Tell me, child.

GIRL: Yes, sah.

BUCHANAN: Do you love me?

GIRL (*promptly*): Yes, sah.

BUCHANAN (*confused by her avowal*): Your mother, now, Daphne by name, I recall as a pleasing creature, with a remarkable expressiveness in the manner of her walking; she would wear a kerchief wrapped about her head like a turban of a gaudy cloth to match her skirt. I believe it served a purpose, she would balance a full wash pail upon her skull and sway beneath it: a sight to gladden tired eyes. Yes. I remember the transaction well: the family of my brother-in-law, the

Reverend Robert Henry, dear sister Harriet's husband, who resided in Greensburg, though his family lived in Shepherdstown, Virginia, was discovered to own two slaves, which fact, if generally known, would certainly disconvenience my public career in the Commonwealth. I had but recently returned from Russia, and Cameron was the king of machinations in Harrisburg. Dallas stood no hope of retaining his Senate seat, but as a peace offering to Governor Wolf I was persuaded to soften my candidacy and yield McKean the prize. What did not meet the eye was this: General Jackson, who could never get enough of Pennsylvanians in Russia, had promised my friends he would next be sending William Wilkins, and I would have *Wilkins's* seat, assuming the anti-Masons and the Whigs refused to band together, as their obstinacy assured, and the Philadelphia faction continued to tar itself with the Bank question. But calculations so delicate could scarcely withstand a slaveholding scandal amid my kin; so by deed of conditional manumission Daphne was assigned her freedom after seven years of service with me, and her daughter would be bound until the age of twenty-eight. And you claim to be she. So how fares your mother then? Ask her if she recalls me kindly, her old Mr. Buck.

GIRL: Dead, sah.

BUCHANAN: What, child? Daphne dead?

GIRL: A soljer beat her, and den she took a fever.

BUCHANAN: Alas. All the best are gone before. Shall I carry her your love?

GIRL (*not comprehending*): Yes, sah.

*Enter* MISS HETTY: Mrs. Johnston is here.

BUCHANAN: I know no Mrs. Johnston.

MISS HETTY: Miss Lane has been married these two and a half years.

BUCHANAN: Oh. Oh dear. I always knew, some folly would claim her. High spirits are ever a treachery, better to be born dull. Better to be dead in the cradle like my sister Mary, died to make room for me in this world. We used to visit, my mother and I, her grave on the ridge at Stony Batter. Mother's skirts rustling by my ear, a little red sandstone with something scratched I couldn't read, it could have been me, it should have been me. (*prays*) Dear Lord, forgive me.

HARRIET LANE JOHNSTON *enters. Contemporary journalists strained to do justice to her "firm, quick step and round, elastic form," to her golden-brown chignon, to "those deep violet eyes, with the strange dark line around them." Orphaned at nine, she became the most popular First Lady since Dolley Madison. Clubs, cravats, flowers, and a government cutter were named after her; the song "Listen to the Mocking Bird" was dedicated to her. Nathaniel Hawthorne, in England early in 1855, met the Ambassador and his niece and wrote: "Miss L—— has an English rather than an American aspect,—being of stronger outline than most of our young ladies, although handsomer than English women generally, extremely self-possessed and well poised, without affectation or assumption, but quietly conscious of rank, as much so as if she were an Earl's daughter. . . . I talked with her a little, and found her sensible, vivacious, and firm-textured, rather than soft and sentimental. She paid me some compliments; but I do not remember paying her any." She brings a harsh vitality to the deathbed.*

HARRIET: What, Nunc? Still playing possum? The day they pulled my baby from my loins, I rose that afternoon and brewed Mr. Johnston some hot rum tea. You men, you play at suffering as you play at war! Here, carry one of these in your belly for nine months if you're tired of dying. (*She hands him a swaddled baby.*)

BUCHANAN (*looking baby in the face*): Mary? (*studies it longer, then exclaims:*) Satan! (*Drops the doll in horror. It stays where dropped, beside him on the bed.*)

HARRIET: Enjoy the flesh, Nunc; it doesn't hang forever on your bones. Get up and play with me. Ellie Reynolds has come over with the Gable sisters and we want to play Texas and need somebody to be Santa Anna for us to throw apples at!

BUCHANAN: Oh, take care, lest you be misled. Folly courts sin, and sin will wed disaster. Believe an old man, Harriet; my heart snapped within me when I was twenty-eight. Those little crabapples could take out an eye.

HARRIET: Get up, Nunc, it's no fun without you! Why are you always indoors writing? What are you writing now?

BUCHANAN: I am composing a cautionary letter to President Polk on the Oregon question. He would plunge us into war with the British over the territory north of the 49th parallel, territory no one in this administration or any of the previous has ever had any sane expectation of securing. Aberdeen and Pakenham are thirsting to settle at the 49th parallel, Congress will turn whichever way the mob shouts, the nation has no more stomach for battling with the British, we must save our war machinery against the impending conflict with Mexico; nevertheless this pinch-mouthed hillbilly Polk has raised the cry of 54° 40′ and his honor now can only be saved by carrying our pose into the very jaws of the lion, then backing away with a grateful bow. As his Secretary of State, I will be delegated to argue the extreme to gain the middle. And, between you and me and the bedpost, dear Harriet, once the settlement is secure, I intend most noisily to place myself among the 54° 40′ men; since the panic for Andy Jackson seized Pennsylvania and left the Federalists with scarce a breechclout to hide their nakedness, no otter has been smoother than your Uncle Jim at riding the mud of popular enthusiasm. Ha! Let the Tennessean founder on his own swashbuckling; in '48 a man of sense will be the candidate!

HARRIET: Just listening to you makes my head hurt, Nunc. When can I go to my first ball?

BUCHANAN: When propriety and nature together dictate. Man is an animal, but a social animal. Society for its manifold blessings asks in exchange sacrifice and compromise. Concession is the world's walking gait. Fevers and hallucinations sweep over us, it is true; but be they permitted to infect the public body, slaughter shall result. Government is either organized benevolence or organized madness; its peculiar magnitude permits no shadings.

HARRIET (*cuddling closer*): But, Nunc, if I can't go to a ball, can I go for a hayride? The Stoltzfus boys keep asking me. They ask me a lot of things.

BUCHANAN: Let them ask unanswered.

HARRIET: But, Nunc, I'm *grow*ing. Something is happening to me in*side*. I can *feel* it.

BUCHANAN: Feel it, but ignore it. Dances, hayrides, your feelings—you are no savage, veto these petitions. My little Hal, you are in the grip of a corporeal conspiracy to have you mate. Why would the unseen conspirators bring you to this? To produce more victims. Life is blind; but the human brain, in the workshop of the Almighty, has forged dim eyes, with the which to foresee a few paces ahead. Look before you leap. Better no marriage than an unfortunate one. Go to your room and read Sir Walter Scott. Next time a hayride is suggested, tell the Stoltzfus boys your uncle wishes to come along and handle the horsewhip.

HARRIET: But the earth is suddenly a honeycomb heavy with secret fragrances. The clouds, the apple blossoms press upon my skin and their impossible kindness leads me to yearn for something impaling, like death.

BUCHANAN (*sitting up sternly*): Be silent. I have heard such things before. The forest once spoke to me also.

HARRIET *flings self on bed, frantic:* Nunc, let me live!

BUCHANAN: In measure. (*He turns away. In turning his head he faces a dark, choleric, powerful man,* ROBERT COLEMAN.)

COLEMAN: Die, Buchanan.

BUCHANAN: Mr. Coleman, sir. I loved your daughter gravely.

COLEMAN: Aye, that's well spoken: loved her so gravely you harried her into the grave. And then, by all that's glorious, had the infernal gall to send me this fawning, weaselling letter. (*reads*) "You have lost a child, a dear, dear child. I have lost the only earthly object of my affections, without whom life now presents to me a dreary blank." Dreary blank, is it? Ye stared for fifty more years, ye consummate hypocrite. "My prospects are all cut off"—thinking of his prospects, and the poor lass still warm in the coffin—"and I feel that my happiness will be buried with her in the grave. It is now no time for explanation"—no, I dare say, nor will there ever be, when there's none but does discredit to the explainer—"but the time will come when you will discover that she, as well as I, have been much abused. God forgive the authors of it." Aye, and God forgive the penman of such an impudent forgery of heartbreak. Courted the virgin child to get a purchase on my fortune, and no sooner did she lay stone cold than he set about courting *me*. Listen to this craven effrontery: "I would like to follow her remains to the grave as a mourner. I would like to convince the world, and I hope yet to convince you, that she was infinitely dearer to me than life. I may sustain the shock of her death, but I feel that happiness has fled from me forever. The prayer which I make to God without ceasing is, that I yet may be able to show my veneration for the memory of my dear departed saint, by my respect and attachment for her surviving friends. May Heaven bless you, and enable you to bear the shock with the fortitude of a Christian." (*to* BUCHANAN, *thunderously*) May Hell damn you, and roast your parsimonious soul to the blackness of a chestnut forgotten in the fire!

BUCHANAN (*feebly, frightened*): You must permit me to explain. There was a misunderstanding—

COLEMAN: No. I understand you well, Buchanan. You are a traitor to your bones. Whatever you touched in your life, you betrayed. Betrayal was your essence, as the snake's essence is venom.

JOHN SLIDELL (*entering from left*): I second that. (*He comes forward to join the deathbed party, which has become a tribunal. The animated pen of Murat Halstead described* SLIDELL *as he looked at the Charleston Convention of* 1860: *"a gentleman with long, thin white hair, through which the top of his head blushes like the shell of a boiled lobster. The gentleman has also a cherry-red face, the color being that produced by good health, and good living joined to a florid temperament. His features are well cut, and the expression is that of a thoughtful, hard-working, resolute man of the world. . . . a matchless wire-worker, and the news of his approach causes a flutter." His Louisiana accent is an overlay; his first twenty-five years were lived in New York City.*) Permit me to introduce myself, the name is John Slidell. (*as he shakes hands*) Special emissary to Mexico under President James K. Polk, Ambassador to France from the Confederate States of America under President Jefferson Davis. Soldier, Senator, mastermind, if you'll allow me, of the nomination of this decrepit rascal for the highest office in the land. Since 1840, let me assure you, he'd been oozing his way after the prize; it slipped from his grasp every four years, sure as leap year came calling. I devised the winning strategy. What *was* that winning strategy? Hide yourself, Buchanan, and trust to the South. *Hide* yourself in London while Bleeding Kansas stains Pierce and Douglas beyond redemption; hide yourself in Lancaster while Southerners hawk Union soothing spirit all over the North. His own state of Pennsylvania, ladies and gentlemen, squeaked through on the speeches of Howell Cobb of Georgia—

JOHN FORNEY (*emerging into the light*): And bales of naturalization papers in Philadelphia.

SLIDELL: The South made him President. They took him for one of their own. Since his first term as a watery-legged mooncalf in the lower house of Congress he played the parasite on Southern political genius. So how did this Judas expunge his debt? He turned his back when the chits were called in. Had he not thrown Floyd to the ravening pack of abolitionist hellhounds, had he treated with the South Carolina commissioners as the man of honor he never was, mobs of the dead would be living still, and two prosperous nations would occupy the territory of a ravaged and bitter Union. You say traitor to your daughter; I say traitor to his party, his true friends, and his own professed convictions.

BUCHANAN: I never claimed slavery was no evil; I merely claimed for it the constitutional protection the framers unambiguously specified. The Constitution above all—

FORNEY: Above all, Jimmie Buchanan and survival. (*Forney: in the steel engraving bound into a book of his dispatches in 1867, a pouchy face with bushy long Burnsides, a self-important brow, a generous nose, a thin and petulant mouth. In the letters from him to Buchanan that fill boxes in the archives at the University of Pennsylvania, an increasingly illegible, almost crazed, scrawl. He must have written many of them while drunk. He is drunk now. Yet he imposes and threatens, and in his own life showed surprising durability, enjoying twenty years as Philadelphia editor and friend of the mighty after his bitter break with Buchanan in 1857. After twenty years of touting Buchanan, twenty of virulent side-switching, backing Douglas, then Lincoln, deserting Andrew Johnson when convenient, and ending as a Democrat again. A messy chameleon, who now imitates Slidell.)* Permit me. John W. Forney, past editor of the Lancaster *Intelligencer,* presently head and owner of the Philadelphia *Press* and *Daily Morning Chronicle.* Miss Lane, congratulations upon your nuptials. Mr. Slidell, you look rosy, the Gallic cuisine must be agreeing with you. Mr. Coleman, we never met, though we've drunk from the same wellspring of treachery. Mr. Buchanan, I disdain to touch your hand. For twenty years, the prime twenty the Good Lord vouchsafed to me, I slaved for your advancement, poling the dainty skiff of your career through the swamp of Pennsylvania politics. When I cried out "Strike!" you sipped Madeira; when I begged you "Speak" you wrote those spidery missives that hedged a hundred ways and faded to nothing in the sunlight. You left it to me, *me* to sink hip-deep in the muck, flailing out at the Know-Nothings, countervailing the intrigues of Dallas and his usurious pack of snobs, not to mention that unspeakable lone skunk Cameron, who bribed his way into *my* Senate seat, when I had reduced my loved ones to destitution so you could wolf partridge in the White House! *(He has worked himself up into a tearful rage.)*

BUCHANAN: Forney, you never learned that every man has his

case, and his price. There are no enemies in politics, only potential allies.

FORNEY: And by the same devil's aphorism, no friends, only tools to be cast away. (*approaches the bed closer*) I nursed your fame with my blood. Each quadrennium, Buchanan, I wrestled forward your name to the verge of the Presidency, and each four years you cowardly squandered the golden opportunity . . .

BUCHANAN: My time had not come.

FORNEY: You fastidious harlot: you let Van Buren steal for New York Pennsylvania's deserved place at Jackson's right hand. You withdrew without a fight in '44 for a place in Polk's Cabinet. In '48 you finagled with the Hunkers and the Barnburners when a firm stand either way might have been the lever to upset Cass; in '52 Marcy might have swung if the right bait had been dangled—

BUCHANAN: Illusions, Forney, illusions. I was beaten every time. The Keystone State was ever a slippery stepping-stone.

FORNEY: And when, sir, in '56, the prize was yours, and all the patronage from Maine to California at your disposal, how was the faithful slave rewarded? With a Cabinet post? By no means. You considered Whigs and Freesoilers, but not your faithful slave, your own right hand. (*gestures imploringly with his right hand*) Then I begged, amid the tears of my five children I begged, for the editorship of the Washington *Union;* certainly, thought the deluded servant, such a lowly piece of jobwork could be mine. How was this entreaty received? With a shut door and the humiliating offer, the naked banishment, of the consulate in Liverpool.

BUCHANAN: The pay was good, the post respectable. You had fouled your own nest, by feuding with the Virginians when you had the run of Washington under Pierce. They told me, only my friendship saved you from extermination in a duel. The Virginians would not have you, and I could not do without *them*. Often I advised you, Forney: build your life upon a firmer base than hope of party patronage.

FORNEY: Upon a firmer base, that is, than service to an ingrate. As it was with me, so with all your good friends from Pennsylvania. Davey Lynch, Johnny Foltz, George Plitt: all betrayed in their moment of triumph—

BUCHANAN: I mourn for you, Forney. I repeat, I mourn.

FORNEY: —betrayed by the coldest-hearted old imbecile that ever sold his friends and his nation into perdition. Mourn for yourself, Buchanan, and for the dead you dispatched through your folly.

ELLIE REYNOLDS, *still a girl, enters, crying:* Mourn for my brother, your best friend's son, killed the first day of Gettysburg. Oh, would that the Rebels had won there, pushed on to Lancaster, and strung your lying carcass from a tree! Oh, die, Mr. Buchanan, please die, and purge me of the hate that rises to gall me whenever I hear your name. (*sobs*)

HARRIET: Ellie? (*puts arms around her*)

ELLIE (*pulling away*): No. You reigned in the White House with him. You were the tyrant's queen.

HARRIET: I did my duty, as he did his, by the light given us. Does power only contaminate? If public office become perforce vile, then none but villains will choose to serve. You came and went in this house as freely as a daughter; you know my uncle to be the gentlest and most circumspect of men.

ELLIE: I know also my brother is dead of a Southern bullet, and that your uncle's Secretary of War, a Virginian, treasonably shipped arms south on the eve of secession.

BUCHANAN (*rising weakly*): Not the case. I cancelled the order the hour I learned of it. The cannon never left Pittsburgh. Floyd was incompetent, not corrupt.

ELLIE: My brother died because the Union was betrayed within Washington. Firm action would have brought the seceders to heel, once Lincoln's election was sure.

BUCHANAN *brushes as if at gnats:* An illusion! Firm action meant the abyss. Inaction was the one last hope. Tranquillize the wavering states, and isolate South Carolina. But Lincoln refused to talk, he stayed in Springfield. He hid behind his party's platform.

SLIDELL: As of course did you, on my advice, four years earlier.

BUCHANAN: But *our* party, then, was the sole bridge remaining between North and South; *his* party had become the very instrument of disunion. In a crisis of such grandeur a gesture transcending party loyalty was called for; but Lincoln did not forthcome. The Republicans were new to power; they clutched it with an infant's tenacity. They scoffed at the apocalypse; they believed that the South, like the grubbing North, wanted utmost to survive, to reap the harvest and hold the profit. But greed can be spiritual as well. There was this they refused to see: a willingness—more, a positive wish—to risk destruction. Lincoln did not know Southerners; I did.

SLIDELL: Then you put the blood on Lincoln's head?

BUCHANAN: No. Once Sumter was fired upon, he became a mere chip on the tide. The Constitution was mercilessly clear. But as long as federal property was not attacked, there was an ambiguity, wherein we could hesitate, and millions could breathe. In this perilous center, for a space of months, I ruled alone. The South and the North beat upon me as two raging oceans, and I held.

SLIDELL: If not Lincoln and his fellow-fanatics, who? Who shall be blamed, if not Garrison and Greeley and Sumner?

FORNEY: Yourself, Slidell, you and Gwin and Toombs and Davis and all those gentlemanly manipulators whose stranglehold on Washington City derived from the barbarous institution of slavery!

BUCHANAN: Forney, you must always fasten on phantoms. Slavery as a method of contracting labor was discredited even in Georgia. Slaveholders yearned for freedom from the slave as earnestly as did slaves from the slaveholder. But the New England agitators had lifted the issue to the level of religion; slavery was forced upon the South as its very soul. Under cover of silence on the question, the South would have slipped its bonds—silence, and the empty courtesy of drawing the Missouri Compromise line through the desert to the Pacific coast.

FORNEY: Silence, and the acquisition of Cuba, and the partition of Texas into four slave states. And then conquer Mexico again, and keep it all this time, as you advised Polk in '48.

BUCHANAN: Dear Forney, you never understood that dreams are made to ease the earth, not replace it. The wealth and power were accumulating in the North; flattery should have been saved for the South. Sufficient unto the day—

FORNEY: You lusted after Cuba, Buchanan, with the lechery a normal man directs toward his concubine. It was the one authentic passion of your reptilian career.

BUCHANAN: —is the evil thereof. Cuba was a factor. All the factors were relative.

SLIDELL (*pressing*): Not Lincoln, not yourself, not us, not them; then who? Who bears the blame? A world in agony cannot be innocent.

BUCHANAN (*with difficulty, sinking deeper into himself*): I could say, but I am dying, and must not be led toward blasphemy.

HARRIET: Ellie, remember the squirrel?

ELLIE *runs to the bed and cries out:* Mr. Buchanan, Mr. Buchanan, Harriet saved a squirrel from the cat but it's hurt, the cat hurt it! What shall we *do*?

BUCHANAN (*kindly*): Amplify your sense of "hurt." Do its hindquarters move?

ELLIE: Oh yes, and its little front paws, just like little gray hands, and it twitches its head with its big bright eyes as if to beg, "Please help me. Please."

BUCHANAN: If its hindquarters move, its back is not broken. All else will likely mend. Place the animal in the washbasket with the lid that has the fasteners of whittled willow; Daphne or Miss Hetty will know which one. Include a saucer of water and a handful of grain from the stables. Do that, and restrain your temptation to take the creature into your hands. A space of calm is the surest cure, if any cure is to be obtained.

ELLIE: We're going to *stone* that cat.

BUCHANAN: No, now, as the rodent is the prey of the cat, the cat is the prey of its own appetites. We mustn't be blamed for our natures, which Providence has bestowed.

*Enter* LAWRENCE KEITT. *He is thirty-six, handsome and sanguine—a prime bloom of Southern chivalry. Waving a piece of paper above his head, he cries:* Thank God! Oh, thank God! South Carolina has seceded, here's the telegram! I feel like a boy let out from school! *(Exit.)*

HARRIET: Get up, Nunc, get up!

BUCHANAN: I have not yet finished my dessert wine.

HARRIET: Get up and play with me!

SLIDELL: Get up, sir, and treat civilly with the South Carolina commissioners. As a plain matter of personal honor you owe them a pledge that the forts will *not* be reinforced.

FORNEY (*a craven, shaken, earlier self* ): Mrs. Forney is very weak, and her infant very feeble. I hope both will be strong enough in a few days, that I may appeal to her once more to yield her objections to my acceptance of the Liverpool position. Like myself, she has built her hopes too high; but unlike me she cannot realize that such hopes are constantly liable to disappointment. I have fallen from complete independence to almost utter dependence and poverty; at a moment when I fondly hoped to assist others, with whom I have been associated for years, I am appalled by the uncertainty of knowing where and how to earn my bread. I find the avenues through which I have spoken with effect occupied by strangers and by foes—men who not only do not care for you but, while preparing to perpetuate their hold upon public patronage after having bitterly opposed your nomination, delight to point to *me* as one whom you have repudiated in your hour of success. Surely I have not deserved this exclusion. In disbelief I learn that Bowman of Bedford has been appointed editor of the *Union*, and Francis Grund, a henchman of Cameron's, in the name of unity has been offered—

BUCHANAN: Enough. You are disunionists, both, and I regret that I have so long listened to your advice.

FORNEY *and* SLIDELL *angrily turn and exit.* ANN COOK *moves across the room, pours more water from the pitcher, and holds the glass to* BUCHANAN'S *lips. He drinks.*

BUCHANAN (*savoring*): A shade tart, but presentable. In Russia, believe it or not, five wines were served with each meal, each in a differently shaped piece of crystal. From immense tureens of solid silver inset with emeralds and rubies they would serve a sour soup that would have repulsed a Delaware Indian. At Peterhoff, amid a wonderful profusion of waterworks fed from the Gulf of Finland, there is a lake, by Peter the Great's little palace of Marly, wherein lives a carp they solemnly assured me to be at least a hundred years old. They had placed a little jewelled collar about its neck and it, with numerous other fish, comes to the edge of the water at the sound of a bell, to receive its breakfast. (BELL *rings.*) Myself, I have fancifully thought, that if there be any truth in the doctrine of reincarnation, I should opt to return as a bullfrog, in such form to reside eternally within my own spring, beside the dusty good red road from Lancaster to Marietta. (*He notices that* ANN COOK *is staring at him.*) Take away that saucy eye, you cocoa wench! A man with my prospects should not be tempted. (BELL *rings again.*)

ELLIE: Mr. Buchanan, Mr. Buchanan! The squirrel is alive! He sat right up and took a biscuit from Harriet's hand!

BUCHANAN: Exactly. Tell Major Anderson to avoid any act which might provoke aggression. The forts for the present will not be reinforced, but he is authorized to take any steps that will increase his powers of resistance.

ELLIE: Oh, Mr. Buchanan, you must be the kindest and wisest man in the entire world!

ROBERT COLEMAN *comes forward and shakes his hand:* Mr. Buchanan, I have heard a great deal of good about you. The word in Lancaster is, you give just value for your fees, and have not been puffed up by your early notoriety.

BUCHANAN (*a younger self, on guard*): If notoriety it is, then I have no cause for self-satisfaction.

COLEMAN: You understand my meaning. The Judge Franklin case was notorious and remains so. And my son George tells me you are defending the Judge once more.

BUCHANAN: I am proud that he has so requested me.

COLEMAN: And yet the bedrock fact is, Houston refused to serve his nation in need, and Franklin merely fined him when he should have been shot.

BUCHANAN: The bedrock fact, from my perspective, is that the Democrats since Jefferson have wished to remove Federalist judges by fair means or foul; and the Houston case, wherein Judge Franklin ruled upon a matter of jurisdiction purely, was a trumped-up *casus dimissio.*

COLEMAN: Are you, then, such a hater of Democrats, Mr. Buchanan? Common knowledge avers that your maiden speech in the Assembly, on the subject of the Volunteer Bill, strayed so far, in its zeal for the poor and for the West, that Billy Beale of Mifflin County then and there invited you to follow your principles into his party.

ANNE COLEMAN (*at his side*): Papa, you do our friend an injustice. His Fourth of July speech that same year indicted Madison so stingingly a printed version was distributed throughout the Commonwealth.

ANNE *resembles the portrait hanging behind her, but animatedly. The long nose, the large dark eyes, the thin mouth quicken to a nervous, willful beauty. She is slender. As in the portrait, a black ringlet spills, with a hint of distraction, across her brow, which is high and white. Her dress has an air of summer: white, high-waisted, of muslin bedecked with blue ribbons, the collar frilled, the skirt unhooped. Sir Thomas Lawrence painted such young women, carelessly pampered and faintly hectic, against dense English greenery and a darkling sky.*

COLEMAN: Forgive me, my daughter, if I venture to assert, in our good friend's company, that that famous speech, though an undoubted masterpiece of demagogic eloquence, seemed to this old warrior in the Federalist cause so severe as to overcarry. The Democrats were not merely criticized, they were expunged from the body politic. Yet no party exists without representing some legitimate interest, and having some weight of good intention on its side.

BUCHANAN (*conciliatory, flirtatious*): I trust you may be pleased to hear, sir, that that same view was expressed to me, in a letter, by my father.

COLEMAN: I have no desire, sir, to duplicate paternal offices already performed.

BUCHANAN: Nor I to have them performed twice. Possibly, on the Fourth of July three summers ago, my youthful desire to strike a memorable stance tempted me to overstate, and to make worse enemies than needed exist. But I have been stung by the aspersions you allude to; I am a Federalist born, and intend so to die. The life of active politics, I may add, recedes in my mind before more domestic hopes.

COLEMAN: Add what you may, the Federalist ship is sinking, young man, and I do not expect you to go down with it. But my daughter's eyes tell me I am acting too much the dragon. Acquaintanceship with you has brought animation into her moods, and this is to your credit, Mr. Buchanan. We shall discuss politics on another holiday. Your cup of cheer is at hand; drink deep of it.

BUCHANAN (*holding his glass of water festively high*): To the Union.

COLEMAN (*not drinking*): Of what?

BUCHANAN: Of all that desire it. But let me amend, rather than be ambiguous. To your constitution, sir; and to the nation's. (*Having drunk, he sinks into sleep, leaving* ANNE *and her father spotlit, with her brother* GEORGE COLEMAN. *Destined to die in three years, at the age of thirty-one,* GEORGE *is tall, stooped, sallow, insinuating.*)

COLEMAN: Your candy man had his section of the Christmas table quite enthralled.

GEORGE: Regaling Mrs. Jenkins, I overheard, with escapades from his student days at Dickinson.

COLEMAN: Has Buchanan ever confessed to you, dear innocent Anne, his derelictions at school? As a present trustee, I have been told they were so persistent and grievous as to warrant expulsion, had it not been for the personal voucher of Dr. John King, then President of the Board.

GEORGE: Worse still, to my mind, than any mere coltish display of bibulousness and swagger, was the incident of the Union Philosophical Society. You know of this incident?

ANNE: I know that Mr. Buchanan was denied the First Honors to which his record entitled him.

GEORGE: Because, my darling sister, he insisted that his Society, against all custom, nominate to the commencement podium not one but two candidates, thereby ousting the rival society from its traditional second place. Well, the faculty's forbearance cracked at that. They gave the first honors to the rival nominee, the second to Buchanan's alternate in the Union Philosophical Society, and the back of their hands to our Jimmy, with the claim that to honor a student so disrespectful would adversely affect student morale!

ANNE: He has confessed to me little love for Dickinson. It is possible, is it not, that small men, running a small college, would hate even incipient largeness, if it appeared by chance among them?

COLEMAN: Or would detest overweening conceit and avarice. Ten years ago, as now, James Buchanan is coldly ambitious, and obsessed by his own advancement. I distrust his purposes thoroughly.

ANNE: One coldly ambitious would have courted the faculty

with circumspection, and blandly received his just due. I know this much about these events, that the entire membership of the Union Philosophical Society, outraged on our friend's behalf, purposed to refuse to speak at commencement, and he dissuaded them.

GEORGE: But to have permitted such a course of defiance would have been a Pyrrhic maneuver. No, Buchanan's bold ploy having failed, conciliation became his only course; and in the end he was allowed to speak, and to receive his diploma along with the honorable and the diligent.

ANNE: You dare say this, when he is renowned throughout Lancaster for those very qualities, of diligence and honor.

GEORGE: A certain quibbling industry, yes. Even a finicking strict adherence to the letter of the law he may be allowed. But a true sense of honor, honor that moves instinctive through a man's being and determines action not by calculation but by instant exclusion of the dishonorable—such a sense of honor is beyond him. He has not the breeding for it. He was born in a cabin, where his father peddled plowshares and whiskey to frontier scum.

ANNE: You speak as if your own fortunate position had been assigned you by a congress of archangels, and did not befall from our father's willingness to gouge the mud for iron. Our comfort is pillowed on the muskets of revolution; this man that you presume to mock has built his name upon a love of law and civilizing order.

GEORGE: My position fortunate?—I, that awake every morning with Death's fingers tighter about my throat? *(One hand about his throat, he comes forward to seize her arm with the other; she shies back.)*

COLEMAN *(protectively)*: Leave off. We will goad her to flight. *(to* ANNE*)* We wish your happiness. If this lawyer pleases, entertain him; but be wary of his suit. Consider, is he intent upon my welfare, or upon my fortune?

ANNE: Father, must I forever be a prisoner of my fortune? I am twenty-three. At such an age my mother your wife had borne two daughters and a son. She too was an ironmaster's daughter, but was allowed to take a woman's role. I tell you, I grow frantic and odd, wasting here, behind the ramparts of your tyrannical self-regard.

COLEMAN *turns away in anger, and exits.*

GEORGE *approaches her closer, insisting:* Buchanan preens upon his association with the Colemans. His manner at law and in the street is quite transformed; he sports new breeches and a russet tailcoat that shimmers like a cock pheasant's feathers.

ANNE: I told him, Walk upright. A man of his prosperity and station should not go about drab as a sexton.

GEORGE: I fear he is advertising wealth to come, not wealth already earned. But if his vanity were lulled by lucre merely, he would be a man easy to read, and easier to lead. Alas, my sweet sister, our Jim has an eye for all manner of allurement. He was seen at the corner of Queen and Vine fairly dancing a jig of attendance on Mary Jenkins and her unwed sister Grace.

ANNE (*laughing*): Is it possible, George, that I comprehend Mr. Buchanan better than you in this respect? I assure you, his innocence would shame a nun.

GEORGE: Innocence can be more dangerous and wanton than experience. I do not think that this attorney, though stout in manner, possesses a heart solid enough for the charge your affection lays upon it. Raw and unchastened, fresh-redeemed from the forest of Stony Batter, he will fancy himself a Romeo, and tread cheerfully upon your pride.

ANNE: My pride does not depend from Mr. Buchanan's behavior. I find your concern impudent.

GEORGE: And I find your folly grievous. Is there no man in Lancaster but this—this squinting mincemouth? (*He imitates Buchanan's deferential tilt of head, and, disloyally,* ANNE *laughs.*) There. Still my pet.

ANNE: No. Never again your pet. You asked me a question: Is there no other man in Lancaster? The answer is, None who so needs me. Without me, he is incomplete. He is afraid.

GEORGE: Afraid of his bid for your hand miscarrying?

ANNE: Afraid of his life miscarrying. Afraid for his soul.

GEORGE: I see. This is his mode of seduction, to present himself as a craven religious—a worm at Heaven's gate. He *is* a worm, and through some pore of your pity has entered your breast, and will eat himself to hugeness. I see. That is why he squints—he is gazing into Hellfire. Poor mincemouth!

ANNE: I regret having even by this little betrayed his trust. You would rend his fineness to spite me.

GEORGE: Your heart is all to me. Buchanan prosper or be damned.

ANNE: Then cease this prying ridicule.

GEORGE (*closer*): My death is here (*strikes chest*). Each night, I say goodbye to life. Each morning, I am less. I have time to love nothing but the sight of you.

ANNE: My life is my own.

GEORGE (*seizes her arm*): I am your brother.

ANNE: Take away your hand. I am your sister, merely.

*As* GEORGE *leaves,* BUCHANAN *groans.*

ANNE *goes to his bedside, sits, touches his arm:* Mr. Buchanan, what does trouble you?

BUCHANAN (*awaking*): Nothing, dear lady. Nothing that the world can cure.

ANNE: You speak slightingly of the world; why? Behold your estate. Your practice each year waxes more profitable; your name is known to the borders of the county and beyond; within Lancaster, you are thought miraculous in the amount of whiskey you can consume while keeping a clear head, and are much admired for the swallow-like ease of your polonaise. (*She gaily demonstrates.*) You are a complete man, Mr. Buchanan, yet you speak with such constant modesty as to arouse suspicion of dissembling. A man who does not value himself will not long be granted estimation in any quarter.

BUCHANAN: Yet are we not, as Bishop Berkeley indicts, creatures all of one another's eyes? Can any existence be said to be self-derived? Parents, teachers, schoolmates, colleagues, rivals: without their surmised opinions, could we distinguish ourselves from air? Are we not each, even those of us so fortunate as to be beloved, each a crossroads of intersecting illusions, with no certain shape but in the eyes of the Maker, who in His mercy leaves us to conjecture what He sees?

ANNE: I cannot follow, but it pleases me to hear you speak with such unaccustomed fire.

BUCHANAN: Consider the Negro—in the eyes of his Southern possessor, a beast of burden fed and guided into usefulness by a missionary solicitude. In the eyes of the Boston anti-slaver, the Negro looms as a white man like himself, a Washington for nobility and a Jefferson for wit, which a mischievous universe has daubed with the tarbrush and hurled into chains. The hapless Negro, hearing the former view more frequently, inclines to conform his manner to it, but also overhears sufficient rumors of the latter to torment him with aspiration. What is he really, we shall not discover in our lifetime, nor in his. Or contemplate Madison's recent farcical skirmish with the British. The ostensible causes for conflict had dissipated before the event, but the event came, and had to be justified, and justified itself, and might have flung us back into subjugation, as an imagined ghost might cause a man of flesh and blood to hurl himself from a precipice. There is, all about us, an empyrean of absolute fact; but human striving agitates it hopelessly, and eventually terms the mud water, and the water mud, and calls the Creator to task indignantly because the earth does not flow, and the ocean will not be walked upon.

ANNE: You sometimes speak as one whose life lacks a center of faith.

BUCHANAN: It lacks it not, insofar as faithful study and prayer can supply it! Forgive me, I presume on your patient attention.

ANNE: I repeat, your fire pleases me.

BUCHANAN: Miss Coleman. May I ask you a question perhaps too personal?

ANNE: I submit to your judgment of what may be borne.

BUCHANAN: In your experience, have you ever—have you ever experienced an inner certainty of salvation? *(Her surprised silence hastens his tongue to elaborate.)* The cry to be saved reverberates throughout the Republic. Revivalists arise in Kentucky, or tramp east from the riverside tents of Ohio, and entreat us to embrace Salvation as if it were an option as plain as risking the first mortgage payment on a parcel of unseen land. And at the camp meetings hundreds cry that Jesus has entered them and their souls are born anew. A swarm of physical symptoms accompany their conversions, and the evidence of my eyes assures me that the churches prosper; the steeple of Trinity Lutheran hoists itself higher than any other structure above the slate roofs of Lancaster. I have reason to suppose that the bulk of my fellow countrymen are possessed by Jesus, whose spirit dwells within them as animatedly as a dragonfly freshly swallowed by a bullfrog. Yet within myself I detect no motions save the pulsing of my heart, the seething of my digestive organs, and the maneuvers of my mind as it seeks to grasp a legal distinction or to locate the nub of a practical affair, and—if I may venture to say—a certain dissolute warmth when I find myself proximate to those who encourage my humors and appear to view my person with favor. But evidently a light blazes in others where my wick remains black. I am in earnest to discover if this be so; yet have no ready method but to invite your kindness, or your mockery.

ANNE: I would never mock you, sir. But, as you profess ignorance of the sensations of others, so must I puzzle my way toward this sensation of yours. Do you doubt that God created the earth and all its wonders? How else could they come to be, save through personal Creation?

BUCHANAN: No, I do not doubt. A first cause must precede the linkages of causation that Nature weaves about us (*gestures outward*) in every tree, vine, and flower of this teeming forest.

ANNE: Do you doubt, then, that the benevolent Agency of Creation, seeing the creature formed after His own image sunk deep within the vile consequences of Father Adam's defiance, did send His Son to teach among us, and to weep, and die—

BUCHANAN: Nay—

ANNE: —to die, and rise on the third day, so that His Resurrection shall forever stand as a sublime indemnity, a rainbow shining in the aftermath of all our storms?

BUCHANAN: Nay, this is not for me to doubt. For there is no tale like it; it wears the magisterial strangeness of actuality, rather than the wistful strangeness of imagination.

ANNE: Then, Mr. Buchanan, why deny yourself the universal absolution? Why not accept the drunken ravings of workworn farmers as true and sufficient evidence? Why resist the helpful pratings of the clergy? Bow your head on the seventh day, and serve the dollar on the other six. Believe, if it make you effective, that a transcendent Presence waits to welcome us when we have stumbled through our little game of blindman's bluff. With you, I fear, the blindfold has slipped a little, and you glimpse the abyss at your feet. (*recites*)

> "I had a dream, which was not all a dream.
> The bright sun was extinguish'd, and the stars
> Did wander darkling in the eternal space,
> Rayless, and pathless, and the icy earth
> Swung blind and blackening in the moonless air."

ANNE *laughs giddily, a momentary demon.* BUCHANAN *studies her.*

BUCHANAN: Then you have been contaminated by Lord Byron's unbelief, as well as his morbidity.

ANNE: I did not need Byron to frame my doubts; I needed him only to show the splendor that is left, when man stands alone amid the cliffs.

BUCHANAN: One or two may strike such a pose; but what of the millions of lesser, bound to drudgery and narrowness, with no consolation save an unearthly one? Dear Anne, you appall me. In the midst of our love, you disclose a chasm. Tell me you merely tease, to draw me out.

ANNE: You are a man, Mr. Buchanan. I will not insult you by pretending to be other than I am.

BUCHANAN: I confess, yes, there is this to say, that were I told, beyond appeal, that the abyss is the substance of truth, I might find rest. But the possibility chafes me, that this God, who freely prattles to children and to criminals on the cross, imposes His silence uniquely upon *me*. Why? The verdict is plain, but I heard no deliberations. Why has He turned his back?

ANNE: You are a man. I am lower than that, a woman. I cannot be concerned with storming Heaven when my father's wealth and your destiny hang so heavy over me.

BUCHANAN: My destiny. Have I one?

ANNE: You do. Instead of a blessing, you have a destiny. That I know. What I do not know is—

BUCHANAN: Come, speak. You have frightened me to my capacity, and can do no worse.

ANNE: —whether or not I am part of it.

BUCHANAN: Dear lady, no one could touch me as you have. I vow, I will carry your image with me to the grave.

ANNE: Let us speak rather of the little portion between the grave and here. You do not know me, Mr. Buchanan. You know me by my appurtenances—as the wearer of my clothes, the dancer of my dance, as the sister of my brothers, the daughter of my father . . .

BUCHANAN: Then the malicious gossip of the town has affronted your ears as well as mine. I will not plead a defense. If your heart is not already fortified, I have built no case there.

ANNE: You build well, Mr. Buchanan, but slowly. The foundation of your case was laid when I was thirteen and from my window on King Street I would watch you pass—young Jamie Buchanan from Mercersburg striding to make his mark in law. The set of your shoulders and the tilt of your head fitted an intaglio already here. (*touches breast*) Any bachelor in Lancaster County might have been mine, in the ten years since, but I bid my heart lay fallow, and I fear it has grown strange. Tell me, am I ill-favored? (*stands, preens, agitated, vexed*) Or is it that you seek a larger fortune? Which of my father's mansions would be yours? Elizabeth Furnace? Cornwall? Martic Forge? Colebrookdale?

BUCHANAN: Why do you goad me?

ANNE: Because, ungoaded, you stand stock still, like a horse before his stall, though it brims with green hay. What holds you back? Marry me. (*She sits upon his bed.*)

BUCHANAN: Your family does not love me.

ANNE: Their love is not at issue. Once announce this engagement, they will put a face on it. Cease cringing before these blacksmiths, Jim; you are destined to leave them behind. From your final height you will look down and wonder where in Penn's overgrown woods the poor Colemans are hiding.

BUCHANAN: Your dreams make me dizzy. I had hoped to win your father's favor before—

ANNE: There is no winning it, save by not seeking it. Your obsequities merely feed his coarse pride, while your successes within Lancaster stir my brothers to ironical envy.

BUCHANAN: Still, time can only accustom them to my attendance, and haste would confirm their suspicions of bad faith.

ANNE: Haste! We first rode out together, to give Molton and Eliza a companion couple, in the blaze of fall. Now the trees are in full green leaf; this summer marks our fourth season of friendship. Are we not ripe? It is no flattery of me, that your courtship moves so circumspectly. They curbed your spirits too hard, perhaps, at Dickinson.

BUCHANAN: Anne, turn away your harsh side. I long for the haven of marriage. The journey has been arduous and solitary, since the days when I watched my father heave up kegs of nails, and crouched within the woodshed to see the drovers brawl. They would fight, in the rage of drunkenness, to the losing of an eye or ear; the howls of men turned animal still come to me, so freshly I think they are under my window, in that muddled clairvoyant interval before we succumb to sleep. This proud nation is but one integument removed from primal savagery; the appurtenances, as you say, of comfort and civility that have been yours since birth are to me a precariously attained realm. Merciless with himself, my father worked us east from the wilderness, east from Cove Gap to the farm in Mercersburg, that seemed Paradise when as a child I was brought there—

ANNE *smiles and quotes:* "The wilderness yielded to the hand of agriculture, and fields loaded with the richest harvests covered these gloomy forests, where wild beasts, but a few years before, had used to roam. Happy, indeed, were this people, had they but known their own happiness." Do you recognize the words?

BUCHANAN: From my own Fourth of July speech.

ANNE: My favorite passage. I can feel there, the child you were.

BUCHANAN: And who still abides with me. My father, at sacrifice to himself, has seen me settled in this chaste and thriving city of Lancaster. I fear to trespass here. I fear you, dear gentle Anne. You urge decision in a delicately balanced world. Let us force no event that gradual causes will in time render inevitable.

ANNE: It is true, what my brothers say. You are cold.

BUCHANAN: No, warm, so warm I feel danger flowing from me like lava. (BELL *rings.*) Since infancy, left to roam alone in the forest about the Cove Gap clearing with no surety but a bell hung about my neck, I have felt the presence of Another, who has his kingdom within as without. Without, this Other sets earthquakes against our shelters and plagues against our bodily frames. Within, he urges blind imperatives, that measure no consequence.

ANNE: If all men so overmeasure, all action will be stillborn.

BUCHANAN: All action, I am convinced, partakes of the nature of sin. Yet an allotment of sin has been set aside for each of us; and in the margin of this mercy we may jubilate, feed, drink, procreate, and strive to outdo our fellows. But make no mistake: our allotment must be spent with parsimony, else the Other within will merge with the Other without, and the shell of social order will dissolve, and the darkness will be as in your poem total.

ANNE: You speak theologically, but as one who accepts the stringencies, and spurns the bounties.

BUCHANAN: As you speak atheistically, yet spurning the terror, and embracing the freedom. You lead me to an abyss, yet are angelically gay and benevolent.

ANNE: I am not an angel, nor am I property; I am a woman. I grow stale in the company of brothers. I wish to be fertile.

BUCHANAN: Dear Anne, you run toward what will come to you. Indulgent wealth, perhaps, has shortened your patience.

ANNE: Always you see me garbed in wealth, Mr. Buchanan. Look at me naked. (*She rips her bodice so her breasts show. Shocked, he turns his face away. Long wait while he turns his head back and dares gaze.*)

BUCHANAN (*smiling*): How mournfully lovely. The imagination, gnashing in its narrow bachelor bed, cannot conceive the truth of it. Such beauty brings me, by a bound, closer to death. My eyes smart. I should weep.

ANNE: Yet you are smiling.

BUCHANAN: I smile because ideality is so tenderly mixed with earth. Your hands grasp; your lips chew; you are shaped to make milk. I am minded twice—of a gallery of marbles such as we see engraved in Latin texts, and of a barnyard. You are a goddess; you are a mammal.

ANNE: Poor Jim, must you ever see each thing twice?

BUCHANAN: It is a lawyer's way.

ANNE: Touch me. That will be single.

BUCHANAN: Have I the right?

ANNE: Here in this forest, there is no polity but consent. The animals and the Indians have been banished by the farmer's musket; the eye of heaven is veiled by leaves. Touch me, but lightly.

BUCHANAN: I am afraid. We are not alone. There is another, who will weight this trespass with fatality.

ANNE (*takes his hand and brings it to the side of her neck*): We are alone.

BUCHANAN *is silent.*

ANNE: Through all this, you love me, I know.

BUCHANAN: Yes. (*At arm's length he touches her shoulder, throat, breast.*)

ANNE: Now we are plighted.

BUCHANAN: We are.

ANNE: Still, do you feel brought close to death?

BUCHANAN: I feel, within, a sweet collapse. There is a darkness I have always dreaded, where most men freely swim. You bring me to its verge. I am grateful.

ANNE (*hunching, chilled*): Do not be. *Life* is the gift I intend, not death. Laugh, Jim. Rage. Assault me. Anything but this regretful gazing. You make me feel naked to my bones.

BUCHANAN: We have made our commitment. Let us pray for its vindication.

ANNE: Your touch grows heavy. (*removes his hand, kisses it*) You are right. The world demands our return. (*gathers torn bodice*) If I am asked, I will say that a thornbush importuned me to be its bride. (*to him, firmly:*) Mr. Buchanan, you see more clearly than I. From this moment forward, I shall trust to your wisdom, and to your discretion.

BUCHANAN (*attempting to josh, her sternness unnerving him*): Better trust to your own proud spirits. The apron of obedient frau, I fear, will not tie easily about your waist.

ANNE (*stung, earnest, leaning closer into the bed and setting her hands over his*): I am not fickle, though you may wish me so. That there is something precarious about me, I grant; but do not mistake my attachment, it is secure. In this neat and self-pleasing place of Lancaster, we have opportunity for few ideas, and must live for those few. There is but one sun in my sky, Mr. Buchanan.

BUCHANAN (*still hoping to joke*): You would make me a sun, when I am a moon.

ANNE: You are my heart's light. I beg you, do not betray me. Though we grow gray and feeble together, I do not expect to beg again. (*turns to go*)

BUCHANAN: Is that the way home? (BELL *sounds.*)

ANNE: My instinct tells me, from this clearing in any direction, the path is sadness. (*She leaves.*)

BUCHANAN *groans.* MISS HETTY *comes to the bed.*

MISS HETTY: Mr. Buchanan, do you have discomfort?

BUCHANAN: No more than is my due, for living so interminably. I imagined I heard the bell downstairs. Is Mr. Swarr coming?

MISS HETTY: In the morning early.

BUCHANAN: What is the hour now?

MISS HETTY: Midnight.

*Enter* JASPER SLAYMAKER *and* JOHN REYNOLDS, *young men about Lancaster.*

SLAYMAKER: Buck, it's early yet; one more swig to see you home.

BUCHANAN: I must appear in court at York tomorrow noon. A tedious number of titles ask to be disentangled for transfer. This spring, there were only purchasers; this fall, there are only sellers. It turns us bankers and lawyers into whirling dervishes, and all the profits turned promissory.

REYNOLDS: There's but one sort of seller worth its salt, and that's a wine cellar. (*holds up glass of water, studies*) Immutable elixir! The blood of gods. (*gives glass to Buchanan*)

BUCHANAN: My kidneys will rebel. (*sips, nevertheless*)

REYNOLDS: You lascivious stoat, don't plead the court in York to us, we know the courting you conserve your manhood for these harvest days. She must be a trim sheaf to gather in (*putting on "Dutch" accent*), ain't that right, Jasper?

SLAYMAKER: At least the hypocrite has the grace to blush.

BUCHANAN: It is the flush of wine.

SLAYMAKER: Brandy by the barrelful never stained your cheek before. (*studies, mock-doctor, Buchanan's cheeks, eyes*) Though the effects are ruddy, the cause is fair.

REYNOLDS: She is *fair,* but when her brothers' eyebrows lower and threaten rain.

SLAYMAKER: Perhaps they see another coming to *reign* in their place.

BUCHANAN: Chaff me to death, but leave my dear betrothed unsullied. You abuse a contented man's good nature. *(Yet he is flattered.)*

REYNOLDS: I wager she is dainty in the proving but difficult once proved. They say the measure of a good match is when the groom trips her up, can he encircle the bride's bare ankle with his hand. Tell us, Buck, is the measurement made, and the maid measured?

SLAYMAKER: Or did you try another yardstick?

REYNOLDS: Yardstick! The man is more than buck; he is a bull.

BUCHANAN: I will tolerate no more. I will get up. *(tries to, but cannot)*

SLAYMAKER *(to Reynolds)*: An empty threat. Until he sees the bottom of a bottle, he is blind.

REYNOLDS: And it takes all of Lancaster to feed him. Have you heard he dines often at the board of Mrs. Jenkins?

SLAYMAKER: Ah, a proven investment.

REYNOLDS: Banker Jenkins might be advised to pay her more *interest.*

SLAYMAKER *(tapping the stony Buchanan's chest)*: He fails to give rise.

REYNOLDS: What is your diagnosis?

SLAYMAKER: Slain by surfeit of pleasure.

REYNOLDS *(to audience)*: Thus spaketh Doctor Makeslayer, who makes well what he cannot slay. *(of Buchanan) Requiescat in pace* this poor tool, whoremonger among the ironmongers, blunted at last by overuse.

SLAYMAKER *(recites)*:


"For the sword outwears its sheath,
    And the party underneath
Cries out, 'You buggering pest,
    Let Love itself have rest!'"

BUCHANAN's *composure cracks; he laughs:* Now I believe it; out-rageousness, persevered with obstinately enough, invades the sublime. (*lifts glass in toast*) To Bacchus, Priapus, and Rufus King. (*drinks*) Now I must make my departure. (*tries to leave bed, looks around in surprise*) I cannot rise. (*tries again*) I am physically unable to elevate my frame. (*All three laugh uproariously.*)

*Enter* MARIA BUCHANAN YATES, *in a bonnet, a-bustle, a pushy plump worried little woman:* Jimmy, get up. The family's all in such fearful trouble—poor Momma dead, Harriet's husband the Reverend Henry dead, dear Jane in Mercersburg coughing blood, Harriet herself so poorly, all those children about to be orphans . . . Whatever are we going to do?

BUCHANAN: Moderation in personal life, dear Maria, plus financial prudence and constant prayer, will equal sufficient solution to every terrestrial care. Since Eden this earth was never intended to be an abode of happiness, it is a place of trial.

MARIA: Well, that's all very well for you to say, the eldest son and all, with your fine big house right on King Street that used to belong to the Colemans and you not in it half the year, having a high time down in Washington with all them fine Southern belles, giving your proud speeches against the Bank and Nick Biddle and all, while back in Meadville here we sit in a house too small by half, you wouldn't lend us enough to buy a bigger; poor Dr. Yates has to use the front parlor as his office!

BUCHANAN: Were I in your situation, I would not scruple to use that room in such a manner. You demonstrate little grasp of your true circumstances. You have had too many children for your pocketbook, and too many husbands for your health. Worst of all, you purchased a property without first having the title ruled free of every encumbrance.

MARIA: Dear Jimmy, don't be such a lawyer with your own flesh and blood! Blessed little Jessie, that I had by your old schoolteacher Mr. Magaw, God rest him, has a touch of consumption and needs to get away from the Meadville damp, and she needs to be educated though she's none too bright, and out of loyalty to you poor Dr. Yates bet a patient two hundred dollars you'd be made Senator in '33 and lost both the bet and the patient when you didn't get it till '34!

BUCHANAN: Had he asked my advice, I would have confidentially recommended that he bet against me. However, I have made the loss good to your impetuous husband, by subtracting two hundred dollars from the amount outstanding on his indebtedness to *me*. You have my receipt. And where, may I ask, is *your* receipt, my dear sister, for the fifty-dollar remittance I allowed you last month?

*Enter* EDWARD BUCHANAN, *a younger, coarser, darker version of J. B.*

EDWARD: You and your receipts. You and your account books. You hug your fortune to yourself while your kindred spit blood and starve.

BUCHANAN (*amused*): Well, Edward, since you are amassing treasure in Heaven, I must lay up a little on earth. Have you ever lacked from me for a loan, or for sound advice?

EDWARD: Yes, you lend. But you never give, and never forgive a penny's interest. Small wonder your Christian faith is pinched thin and querulous. For it is written, "Easier for the camel to go through the eye of a needle than for a rich man to enter into the kingdom of God."

BUCHANAN: It is also written that the servant who increased his five talents to ten was praised.

EDWARD: "Provide neither gold, nor silver, nor brass in your purses, nor scrip for your journey."

BUCHANAN: "The kingdom of heaven is like unto a merchant man, seeking goodly pearls."

EDWARD: Quote scripture if you will; I know the pit within your heart. You dread death, and flee from solitude. Impious horrors throng your imagination.

BUCHANAN: You should not rebuke me with what I confessed to you as a fault. Had I your vocation, I would be content with your straitened circumstances. Nay, I would rejoice in them, as sure signs of everlasting reward. Edward, I strive to pray, but my mind wanders; devils of mockery insert themselves in the hesitations of my creed. But it is written, consolingly, that our father's house has many mansions; until I am vouchsafed a stronger faith, I must comport myself as an outward Christian, and serve the world.

EDWARD: You serve it with a vengeance. Our sainted mother, foreseeing her death, wrote and begged you to decline the mission to Russia. Ambition beckoned, and you went.

BUCHANAN: Do not chastise me with that. Duty beckoned, not ambition.

EDWARD: Duty of a seductively glamorous and enhancing sort. When our mother prayed her Lord aloud for a son in Christ's ministry, you and George already deep in the lucrative practice of the law, who did his duty then? And when George, still in his prime, his brilliance outshining yours, succumbed to fatal disease, who held his fevered hand and bestowed upon his brow the balm of religious assurance? As he gasped his last, you, whom he loved and admired to the folly of emulation, were dancing in Petersburg with aristocracy's jaded harlots!

BUCHANAN: Envy leads your tongue astray. Tell me, brother, what need occasions your visit?

EDWARD (*with dignity*): In hopes that the name Buchanan enjoy association with concerns more spiritual than the manipulations of diplomacy and politics, I have sought donations in Pequea Parish to endow a chair of theology at some one of the Episcopalian colleges. However, the parish is neither wealthy nor, unlike the Biblical widow, alacritous to part with its mite.

BUCHANAN: What sum did you envisage?

EDWARD: In my temerity, not less than one hundred and fifty dollars.

BUCHANAN: And how much of that is in hand? How much has your parish contributed? (*after silence*) Come, tell me.

EDWARD: Six dollars.

BUCHANAN: Then permit me to pledge a check to the amount of one hundred and forty-four dollars exactly. Will that sufficiently gratify your superiors?

EDWARD: It is not my superiors we seek to gratify, but the One superior to us all, whose accounts will not omit this generosity of yours.

BUCHANAN: I trust not. A clerical error in Heaven is chaos here below.

EDWARD: It distresses me, to hear infidel wit from my brother's lips.

BUCHANAN: And it distresses me, to suffer reproaches from a beggar. Patience, my reverend brother, would more become your professions of concern for my eternal welfare. I am busy every minute with the painstaking labor of dying. The vanities of public success have lost all savor; a bilious affliction has robbed me of the pleasures of the table; the comforts of marriage have eluded me; my prime is past. The day is not far off when you may divide my financial carcass with the hungry multitude of our orphaned nephews, consumptive nieces, and improvident sisters. Until that joyous reckoning, pray do not beat me with your piety, or leech your poverty upon my sores. God safeguard your return to Leacock Township. My check will be in the mails.

EDWARD: Our father was hard, but toil made him so. In you, hardness has become a decadent habit. In farewell I say sincerely, God mend your erring ways, brother James. *(Exit.)*

*Female laughter!* MRS. MARY JENKINS *and her sister* GRACE HUBLEY *are discovered by a change of light at Buchanan's bedside. The married sister is brunette; the unmarried, blonde. Both flirt automatically. Their laughter tinkles like china; their beauty has a brittle pallor. The scene has something in it of clockwork.*

MRS. JENKINS: Some more tea, Mr. Buchanan?

BUCHANAN: The hour beckons me away. But a touch more of such an innocent brew should perform no lasting harm. *(Holds out water glass;* MRS. JENKINS *nicely pours what is also water from the pitcher.)*

MRS. JENKINS: Mr. Jenkins will be bitterly disappointed to have missed your kind call.

BUCHANAN: Merely inform him, if you would, that this most recent of my trips to Philadelphia over the matter has provided encouraging indications that the Columbia Bridge Company suit may admit of a settlement out of court more imminently than a reasonable hope deemed possible. By early December, I would judge. But none of this, needless to say, is for ears other than your loved one's.

MRS. JENKINS: *Need*less to say. I *do* hope it doesn't offend you to have my dear Grace eavesdropping upon our secrets. She *is* my sister, and I can promise you, from more years ago than a gentleman should count, that she is no tattletale! (*female laughter, again*)

BUCHANAN: Offend me, nay; I am greatly gratified. I would not have believed, without the pleasant evidence of this meeting, that the Hubley mint contained enough rare metal to strike two such glittering coins.

MRS. JENKINS (*to* GRACE): Isn't he a perfect delight?

GRACE: I understand from my little sister, Mr. Buchanan, that not only does the fate of Mr. Jenkins's bank depend entirely upon the exercise of your legal talents—

BUCHANAN: I will not be provoked to denial of praise so unlikely.

GRACE: —but that you and he serve together on a committee to advise your Congressman on the Missouri Question.

BUCHANAN: Lancaster is a small city, Miss Hubley, and a few dogs must bark on many streetcorners.

GRACE: I as*sume* you advised him to vote a*gainst* extending slavery to Missouri; oh, I think it wicked, wicked, *wicked*, the way those planters want to spread their devilish institution over all of God's good terrain!

BUCHANAN: We do so advise, though in terms less fervently couched than your own. Myself, since the Constitution undeniably sanctions slavery, I see no recourse but accommodation with it *pro tempore*. A geographical compromise, such as rumor suggests Senator Clay will shortly propose, to maintain the balance of power within the Senate, would, I am convinced, allay the sectional competition that has heavily contributed to this present panic of selling and suing.

GRACE: Oh, I *do* adore men, the sensible way they measure one thing against another. *My*self, I just cannot let my spirit *dwell* on the fate of those poor darkies, the manner in which not only the men but the way the colored ladies down there are abused—un*speak*able abuse, Mr. Buchanan; pure death would be *far* preferred—I can*not*, it is a weakness of my nature, I cannot contemplate such wrongs without my heart rising up and yearning to smite those monstrous slavedrivers into the outer darkness that will be their everlasting abode!

BUCHANAN: You speak as a soldier's daughter, Miss Hubley. Here in peaceable Pennsylvania we traditionally take a less absolute view. The slavedrivers, it may be, are themselves driven, by circumstances they did not create. But I adore, to re-employ your hyperbole, the passion of your good will and the clarity of your indignation. God's design, it is evident, presents no riddles to your vision.

GRACE: What riddles there are, Mr. Buchanan, I leave to the Lord to solve.

BUCHANAN: May I ask—I ask in all respectfulness, with full solemnity—have you had, then, an inner experience of election?

GRACE: I would not express it in so political a phrase. For as long as I can remember, I have sensibly felt the closeness of the Lord. He looks over me, He approves of me, He rebukes me, He enjoys me.

BUCHANAN: How I envy you!

GRACE: But is this not true of everyone? At least, of the white and educated race?

BUCHANAN: You ask, I cannot answer. My own sad case may be singular.

MRS. JENKINS: It is not a woman's way, Mr. Buchanan, to make an issue of doubt. But surely Miss Coleman, to the degree of intimacy that is already your privilege, relieves your anxieties, and charms away your fine reasoning.

BUCHANAN: Alas, gentle ladies, not only does she herself doubt; she mocks. She is a headlong reader of Lord Byron's bombastic and cynical scribblings, and I fear has some sympathy for the most vicious anti-principles of the European revolutionaries.

GRACE: But how can that be? Her family is the richest in Lancaster!

MRS. JENKINS: Dear Grace, you cite as objection the very cause. And consider, how else but by extravagance can feminine spirits dent the world, that rolls on without once asking their advice?

BUCHANAN: But the very perpetuation of the race lies within the power of women. And their domestic labor forms the basis of social order! Surely heartsick defiance need not assert an authority acknowledged by our entire mortal course, from first cry for milk to last cry for—tea. (*sips*)

GRACE: I *so* much agree, good sir. Were I plighted to a man of my heart's disposition, however humble might be his station in life, I would claim myself infinitely content. The suspicion has been raised in Lancaster, has it not, that your relations with Miss Coleman are disadvantaged, given the delicacy of her temperament, by the size of her fortune?

MRS. JENKINS: Really, Grace, you presume.

BUCHANAN (*warned, brisker*): Her fortune indeed complicates our alliance. I would not have offered myself to her regard, had I not by my own initiative accumulated an adequate capital. But so much discussion of the young lady awakens compunction in me. I had meant to stop by only a moment, Mrs. Jenkins, covered with the dust of the turnpike, to give your good husband our hopeful news; and I have betrayed my purpose. Forgive me. Farewell, Miss Hubley. I am tempted to use your first name, since you are as outwardly graceful as inwardly confident in Grace.

GRACE: Oh, stay!

BUCHANAN *does not rise.*

ANNE, *offstage, cries:* Traitor! Traitor!

*Darkness engulfs the ladies and rest of the stage, but for the bed.* ANNE'S *shriek dies into sobbing, fades into the ringing of the* BELL. BUCHANAN *sits up terrified, his white nightgown spotlit.*

*Enter his mother,* ELIZABETH SPEER BUCHANAN, *clad in the coarse undyed homespun of a frontierswoman before the turn of the century.*

MOTHER: Get up, Jamie, get up. The cock has been crowing and badgering his hens for hours.

BUCHANAN (*hugs her*): Oh Mama. I had a bad dream. I dreamt I was lost in the forest.

MOTHER: You kinna get lost in the forest, Jamie, as long as you wear your little bell. (*She puts it around his neck.*)

BUCHANAN: The Devil might hear it before Papa does. Or an Indian. Or a dead man the Indians boiled to death.

MOTHER: Now where's my brave lad? What manner of timid talking is this? The De'il kinna set his hand upon ye, if your heart be in the holy state. As to the Indians, if ye're ascared of a red savage or two or three, how can ye be a soldier with General Washington, when next he marches west to battle the Whiskeymen?

BUCHANAN: I get afeerd in the woods.

MOTHER: Then stay close in the cabin and help me mind the little ones. Or else go help your father load the pack trains. Nobody leads you to those woods but you, Jamie Buchanan.

BUCHANAN: Was it the Devil got little Mary?

MOTHER: Ah, 'twasn't the De'il but his opposite, a death angel of the good Lord took little Mary off to be with Himself. And the same Lord sent us yourself, and little Jane, and sweet Maria here to take the baby's stead. (*She lifts the swaddled baby doll, fetched in by* HARRIET, *from where it has lain neglected on* BUCHANAN's *bed.*) Think ye the De'il could have a hand in such a marvel? Oh, now doesn't he wish he could? (*clasps baby to bosom, rocking it as she says to her son:*) Jamie, Jamie, never you forget what I am telling you now; never forget it though you grow to be a great old man. Whene'er the Devil thrusts his fear into yer heart, dinna run, for ye're as apt to hasten deeper into trouble as make it safely off. Rather than any o' that, you stand you still and say your prayers. Old Nick is a mighty lad but he can't stand up to a prayer from the soul; and in all God's green world he's the only one to give us a hurt we can carry beyond the grave. (*She unbuttons her bodice and suckles the infant. Noticing* BUCHANAN *watching too intently, she says:*) Now get up, Jamie lad, and give us a kiss. (*She holds forward her face to be kissed, while still holding the baby to her breast.*)

BUCHANAN: No. No kiss.

MOTHER: Then get up, boy, and be about your business.

BUCHANAN (*harder*): No.

*The light around the bed widens, disclosing others in attendance.*

HARRIET: Nunc, get up! The Prince of Wales is coming, and he will want to dance with me!

BUCHANAN: No. There will be no dancing at the White House.

Methodists from Maine to Georgia would cry that the Devil has taken possession of Washington City. Many think so already.

HARRIET: But our old friend Victoria will say we didn't give her little boy a good time.

BUCHANAN: Little boy indeed, short of nineteen and an accomplished whoremaster. My spies assure me not a *poule* in Canada has been left unruffled by his continental visit; and now the lubricious Prince would descend with his retinue of toadies into the innermost nest of republican virtue. Lechery! That's why Europe teeters on the glittering verge of the abyss, while Nebraska grain grows tall wherever a white man steps! Placate your rhythmic itch elsewhere, dear Harriet; patent leather polished by the sweat of colonized coolies shall never twinkle on carpets made sacred by the Protestant pacing of Taylor and Tyler, Fillmore and Pierce!

HARRIET: You sound strange, Nunc. Are you weary?

BUCHANAN: Cobb assures me that Georgia will never tolerate the election of Lincoln. I am weary to the bones and beyond. Escort your royal popinjay in the good ship *Harriet Lane* up to Mount Vernon and revel in the nude, for all I care, as long as there's water beneath your bottoms. Only keep your own thighs snug; raddled with syphilis you'll make a botchy Queen of England, no matter what lewd poetry the Prince of Wales employs to lull your defenses. And take your portrait from the Prince's bedroom, lest it drive his left hand to frenzy.

HARRIET: Don't poke fun at me, Nunc. I *so* want to get married.

BUCHANAN (*more tenderly*): Alas, dear child, you are married to me for the duration of our terror. Here I sit ensconced, surrounded by nonsense, by pimpled princes and delegations of Japanese factotums wearing black boxes on their heads and two swords in every belt, while under my brooding a million mourning mothers are being hatched, and the blessed Union being tugged in two by politicians blind as rhinoceri and greedy as shoats! Dear little Hetty, you are all that is left to me of my favorite sister Jane; an entire world lost survives solely in you. Hold off the tyrant venery an interval longer, till we have done performing our melancholy office.

MISS HETTY: Mr. Buchanan, the Charleston commissioners are at the door.

BUCHANAN (*aside*): They do not give me time to say my prayers. (*to her:*) I have determined to receive them, but only as private gentlemen.

SLAYMAKER *and* REYNOLDS *burst in.*

REYNOLDS: Buck, have you heard the news? Anne Coleman has gone to Philadelphia!

SLAYMAKER: She took her sister Sarah to visit her sister Margaret—

REYNOLDS: —the wife of Judge Hemphill—

SLAYMAKER: —whose brief career in Congress earned him the sobriquet of "Single-Speech Hemphill."

BUCHANAN: I had not heard.

REYNOLDS: Are you no longer in communication?

BUCHANAN: There has been a misunderstanding.

SLAYMAKER: Well then, get up and follow her. The wench is begging with her tail for a show of devotion.

BUCHANAN: I believe Miss Coleman to be sufficiently acquainted already with the quality of my devotion. The situation is such that a strenuous protest from me would merely compromise my dignity, without adding a fact to the matter. Further, the Columbia Bridge Company case nears settlement and requires my presence here, at the prothonotary's office.

SLAYMAKER: Buck, you are too cool. She is yours; go claim her.

BUCHANAN: Cool I am not, but I am no mortgage-holder either. Miss Coleman several days ago sent me an offended note, releasing me from our engagement.

REYNOLDS: And you responded how?

BUCHANAN: I am grieved, but have phrased no answer. The nature of her accusations did not admit of a defense, only of the possibility that time and silence will reduce them to their self-evident absurdity.

SLAYMAKER: Is it true, as all the tongues in Lancaster are wagging, that coming back from some days' absence you forthwith called upon Mrs. Jenkins and her sister Grace Hubley and made gay over tea, while Anne awaited your return at Colebrookdale?

BUCHANAN: My business with the Jenkinses had to do, again, with the Columbia Bridge case. My business takes me into many agreeable homes, where I am treated courteously. I am—was—betrothed, yes, but not—I trust—tethered.

SLAYMAKER: Then cast off this prothonotarial tether and gallop to the City of Brotherly Love. You know the lady's taste in literature; be Byronic, for once in your conscientious life.

BUCHANAN: After months of careful labor I have negotiated a compromise that will enable the Susquehanna to be bridged. I will not jeopardize this settlement in order to pursue vain phantoms. Such pursuit in any case would only confirm her suspicions of my avidity. When the ink is dry on the contracts, time enough will remain to soothe the lady's flighty heart.

REYNOLDS: Time enough for a hundred local doxies might not do for a Coleman. The girl is proud.

BUCHANAN: Am I craven then? Let the Colemans learn their place in humanity's ranks. Let Anne outwait her sulk in Philadelphia. Let her buy a few gowns, and see a few comic operas, and in that way dilute with artificial nonsense the nonsense of her cloistered self-regard.

SLAYMAKER: This is not the judgment of a man in love.

BUCHANAN: Judge not how I love. I love in my own guise. I will not don a Turk's costume for this emergency. If our betrothal cannot withstand this mockery of a tempest, it deserves no longer trial.

REYNOLDS: Send her at least a note, confessing shock and sorrow.

BUCHANAN: If I have not offended, why should I make apology?

REYNOLDS: Perhaps you offended, not with your willing intent, but with the unwilling whole of you, in some part hidden from you, yet nevertheless part.

BUCHANAN: I deny the possibility. Relations between persons, between lovers as well as businessmen, between parent and child as between legislator and constituent, must transpire where reason can grasp them. Otherwise an encroaching vagueness descends upon commerce. This nation, and all compacts drawn up as shelter from the superstition and bloodlust of natural men, must function in the light; I will not be drawn into the shadows after Anne. She knows me well enough; she knows what I am, and where I am. I am in Lancaster, and she is safe at Chestnut Street. I will not move. Now leave me, please, to my prayers. (*As he has spoken, darkness has possessed the stage. Almost invisible, he prays.*) Dear Lord, who in the guise of a shepherd redeemed from afar the sheep in one hundred that had strayed, bring back Anne to me. Allow her wit to see through false gossip; allow her love for me to forgive whatever may yet be true in these mischievous allegations, whose authors would be also my comforters. Let her presence, though she doubt Thy goodness, be restored to my flesh, and complete my manhood. That failing, let me accept my solitude as a work of Thy Providence, to be borne in gratitude, as punishment for sin without beginning, and without end. Amen.

BUCHANAN *lies inert, breathing with difficulty: the dying man. Enter* ALEKSANDRA FEDOROVNA, TSARINA OF RUSSIA, *born* CHARLOTTE LOUISE, *daughter of William Frederick III of Prussia. As she approaches the bedside, fluttering a little glistening white fan, she gathers light to herself, in her dazzling wide ball gown; there is a blaze of jewels at her throat, wrists, and head. Buchanan's references to the Empress in his Russian correspondence are few and terse. In a dispatch to President Jackson on June 22, 1832, he wrote, of their first meeting: "The Empress talked very freely. She spoke on several subjects, and with great rapidity. . . . [Of Southern troubles] I endeavored in a few words to explain this subject to her; but she still persisted in expressing the same opinion, and, of course, I would not argue the point." In a letter to Mrs. Slaymaker four months later: ". . . & the gaieties of the season are expected to commence as soon as the Empress shall recover from her accouchement. She is remarkably fond of dancing in which she excels." Next year, on May 19th, he confided to John B. Sterigere: "I think I may say, I am a favorite here, & especially with the Emperor & Empress." His diary notation for the Peterhoff fête (July 13, 1833) recorded: "We went over to the ball about eight in the evening, where the emperor and empress and the rest of us polonaised . . ." And, in his account to Secretary of State Louis McLane of his final audiences in*

*St. Petersburg on August 5, 1833, this paragraph: "I had, on the same day, my audience of leave of the Empress who was very gracious; but what passed upon this occasion is not properly the subject for a despatch." The* TSARINA *approaches gingerly, her wide gown swaying; beneath her rouge and beauty spots she is the actress who plays* ANNE COLEMAN. (*Soft ringing of the* BELL.)

TSARINA: Monsieur?

BUCHANAN: Votre Majesté!

TSARINA: Pourquoi se repose-t-il si tristement, comme une grenouille hors de l'eau, Monsieur l'Envoyé Extraordinaire et Ministre Plénipotentiaire des Etats-Unis d'Amérique, cette belle République où tous les hommes sont égaux, et également libres de se mettre à la poursuite du bonheur? Je pense qu'il a le mal du pays, de son pays chaud et fertile, alors qu'il faut vivre dans notre royaume tellement froid!

BUCHANAN: Non, Votre Majesté, ce royaume, et sa reine surtout, sont très aimables. Aux Etats-Unis, dans mon état natal de Pennsylvanie, les hivers sont froids aussi, mais plus modérément qu'ici. Chez nous, nous aimons aussi les promenades en traineau quand il neige. (*Bells; sleighbells; Buchanan's* BELL.)

TSARINA: Ecoutez! Entendez-vous la musique, Monsieur Buchanan? Elle nous dit, "Dansez! Dansez!" (*It becomes harpsichord music.*)

BUCHANAN: Ah, Madame, je reconnais le son; il touche mon cœur avec mélancolie.

TSARINA: Je vous commande d'oublier votre pays, le pays lointain et enchanté où tous les hommes sont libres et tristes. Il y a un temps pour la mélancolie, il y a un temps pour jouer le rôle d'un ministre très sérieux, il y a aussi un temps pour danser. Voyez-vous l'empereur là-bas? Il nous regarde. Sa

Majesté serait très offensée si vous ne dansiez pas avec son impératrice.

BUCHANAN: Vraiment?

TSARINA: Bien sûr! C'est un devoir diplomatique. Les relations entre votre république et notre empire en dépendent. Le destin du monde en dépend.

BUCHANAN: En ce cas, permettez-moi. (*Against stiff invisible resistance he rises from his bed.* BUCHANAN *stands, in his white nightshirt, arms lifted, offering to dance.*) Votre Majesté.

TSARINA: Monsieur!

*They dance, to an offstage harpsichord, a minuet.*

TSARINA: Vous dansez très bien, Monsieur Buchanan. Peu d'hommes aussi grands que vous le feraient avec une telle grâce.

BUCHANAN: J'ai appris à danser avec Andrew Jackson. Mon Président fait ceux qui le suivent très agiles. Après l'avoir suivi, les pieds sont pleins de la grâce.

TSARINA: Assez de grâce, peut-être, pour vous porter jusqu'à la présidence—comment dîtes-vous?—jusqu'à la Maison Blanche!

BUCHANAN (*laughs*): Mais la grâce seule est insuffisante: il faut aussi la force.

TSARINA: En manquez-vous?

BUCHANAN: Je ne sais pas. C'est un mystère de mon destin. N'importe. A chaque jour suffit sa peine. Je serais heureux de danser avec vous pour toute l'éternité!

TSARINA (*laughs*): Eternellement mon ministre plénipotentiaire?

BUCHANAN: Eternellement votre serviteur, ma Reine de la Neige.

TSARINA: Vous êtes trop flatteur. J'ai peur que vous trahis-
siez . . . (*Waltz rhythm begins.*) Ah, la danse moderne! Mon
beau-père, l'Empereur Alexandre, dansait la valse à Paris
au moment où Napoléon recevait le coup de grâce.

BUCHANAN: Et sans Napoléon, les Etats-Unis n'existeraient
pas! Le pas de valse, c'est simple: suivez-moi. (*shows her how*)

TSARINA *laughs, as the music grows, and they whirl, whitely whirl
together, and her laugh revives, as the Curtain falls.*

# ACT II

*Wheatland has been transformed into the White House by the sub-*
*stitution of George Washington's portrait for Anne Coleman's. The*
*desk before the fireplace, with its chairs, acquires a new importance.*
*The bed is now a podium, bearing a large Presidential seal.* BU-
CHANAN *is up and dressed, in his customary, rather clerical garb of*
*black swallowtail coat, black breeches, shiny black pumps, and snowy*
*high white stock with white cravat. His coat, however, is his famous*
*"Inauguration Coat," which a Lancaster tailor had "lined with*
*heavy black satin, into which was stitched a representation of all 31*
*States, with 'Keystone' in the centre."* HARRIET LANE *wears her*
*Inauguration Ball dress, a white dress "decorated with artificial*
*flowers and . . . necklace of many strands of pearls." He and she are*
*continuing the waltz, to the same harpsichord music and sound of*
*bells.*

HARRIET: Nunc, stop, stop! You're making me ever so giddy!
BUCHANAN: Tush-a-loo, my darling niece. They call you our
    Democratic Queen; weak legs and head never made an

Empress, never mind the ins and outs. Not every fair day of a backwoods boy's life he takes the Presidential oath, his head stamped forever amid the frozen stars and his backside aflame like a saint's pyre with the National Hotel Disease! Ha! (*twirls, displaying inner lining of his coat, with its embroidered array of the coats of arms of the States*)

HARRIET: Really, Nunc; you offend my modesty.

BUCHANAN (*takes her hand seriously; music dies*): I would speak thus only to you. To the rest of the world I say (*goes to podium*): The kind Providence which inspired our fathers with wisdom to frame the most perfect form of Government and Union ever devised by man will not suffer it to perish until it shall have been peacefully instrumental, by its example, in the extension of civil and religious liberty throughout the world.

HARRIET (*looking around*): How dingy it all is! Poor Mrs. Pierce, such an unhappy woman. Everything must be refurbished, and I rather fancy adding a conservatory. (*turns*) Nunc, the Baron de Stoeckl confided to me at the Ball that he found your allusion to the Supreme Court rather enigmatic.

BUCHANAN: All will come clear in a twinkling. The agitation over slavery in the Territories is dead! The Supreme Court is about to announce, thanks to a little judicious pressure (*enacts push, with a dancer's motion*) from me on Justice Grier, who after all occupies the seat on the Court that Polk originally offered to *me*—the Court is about to announce, I say, in connection with the trivial case of one Dred Scott, a sometime slave, and reputedly a shiftless one, to announce that the Congress has no right to legislate slavery from any of the Territories, that the Georgian with his slave may safely range as far and wide as the Vermonter with his mule, that Douglas's poppycock doctrine of Squatter Sovereignty is a slogan devoid of content, and that the Black Republicans' favorite rallying-point has gone the way of the winds! A party without an issue, a nation without a discord! Ha! (*dances to podium*) Most happy will it be for the country when the public mind shall be diverted from this question to others of more pressing and practical importance. Throughout the whole progress of this agitation, which has scarcely known any intermission for more than twenty years, whilst it has been productive of no positive good to any human being, it has been the prolific source of great evils to the master, the slave, and to the whole country. It has alienated and estranged the people of the sister States from each other, and has even seriously endangered the very existence of the Union. Nor has the danger yet entirely ceased. Under our system there is a remedy for all mere political evils in the sound sense and sober judgment of the people. Time is a great corrective. Political subjects which a few years ago excited and exasperated the public mind have passed away and are now nearly forgotten. (*Cheering issues from an applause machine at the back of the theatre.*)

HARRIET: Those hideous mahogany bookcases of Fillmore's have never been filled; we must write Foyle's to ship us English novels by the bushel. Nunc, are you sure the country will be so easily lulled as you say?

BUCHANAN: Law is law, my child. Since the Territorial question was ever nine-tenths an abstract concern, legal abstraction will settle it. Let care be banished from your pretty golden head; Chief Justice Taney and I, two old Dickinson boys, will bring the class to order. All slavery agitation quelled, together North and South will face outward to the horizons: this administration will throw a military road to the Pacific coast, bring the ruttish Mormons to heel, pluck Cuba that emerald jewel from the moribund hand of Spain, and twist the arm of Mexico until she yields up Lower California, Sonora, and Chihuahua as compensation for her insults to the flag! (*opens his coat with its marvellous emblemed lining; cheers*)

HARRIET: But Nunc, won't the New Englanders say you're enlarging the slave territory, to gratify the South?

BUCHANAN: There's no pleasing New Englanders, my dear; their soil is all rocks and their hearts are bloodless absolutes. Not one electoral vote did they contribute to my election. It takes a madman like Frémont or old Quincy Adams to jingle their bones. Give me one amorous promise, before you go to bed: never to marry a Yankee. Nor a daredevil fire-eater either. Marry a man from the Middle States, where sound judgment keeps company with a full stomach. (*takes podium*) We are indeed a nation, confederated with thirty other sovereign nations of States by the most sacred political instrument in the annals of mankind, called the Constitution of the United States. (*cheers*) Pennsylvania is truly the keystone of this vast confederacy, and our character and position eminently qualify us to act as a mediator between opposing extremes. Placed in the center, between the North and the South, with a population distinguished for patriotism and steady good sense, and a devoted love to the Union, we stand as the daysman, between the extremes, and can declare with the voice of power to both, hitherto shalt thou go, and no further. May this Union endure forever, the source of innumerable blessings to those who live under its beneficent sway, and the star of hope to millions of down-trodden men throughout the world! (*Cheers; they die. Stage is dark, but for restless light on* BUCHANAN. HARRIET *has gone to bed.*)

BUCHANAN: I am too uplifted to sleep. The air of this capital buzzes with rumors. The busy bees of power are at work within my chest.

ANDREW JACKSON *emerges from shadows. In the words of Albert Gallatin: "a tall, lank, uncouth looking personage, with long locks of hair hanging over his face, and a cue down his back tied in an eel skin; his dress singular, his manners and deportment that of a back-woodsman." He is played by the actor who played* GEORGE COLE-MAN. *It is the morning of December 30, 1824.*

JACKSON: Young man, come take the air with me, along Pennsylvania Avenue.

BUCHANAN: I would indeed be honored, General Jackson. (*They walk.*)

JACKSON: You tarried this morning, I thought, with a gleam in your eye, as of one with a message to impart.

BUCHANAN: No message, sir, but a question. However, before I pose it, let me petition in advance for a guarantee of your continuing friendship, which I value high above all my claims to public service, saving only my love of the Constitution and the great Christian people that it serves.

JACKSON (*impatience scarcely concealed*): That is well said.

BUCHANAN: My question concerns—and how could it not?— the Presidential election, a subject upon which, typically, and to your great honor, you have expressed a determination to remain silent. I recognize that, deeming the question improper, you may refuse to give it an answer; believe me that my only motive in asking it is friendship for yourself.

JACKSON: Speak on, Mr. Búchanan (*accenting the first syllable, in frontier fashion*). From your high respectability as a gentleman and a Congressman, I do not expect you would lend yourself to any communication you suppose to be improper. Your motives being pure, let me think what I will of the communication.

BUCHANAN (*not quite satisfied, but proceeding*): My question needs little preamble. We live, General, in times of intrigue and rumor; would that we lived in a better, but we do not. A report exists in circulation that, if—as I fervently hope and trust—you are elected President by the House, that you will continue Mr. Adams in his present office as Secretary of State. You will at once perceive how injurious to your election such a report might be. It rises, I think you will also perceive, from the friends of Mr. Adams, as a reason to induce the friends of Mr. Clay to accede to their proposition, which has been distinctly forwarded, that Mr. Adams's election will bring with it the appointment of Mr. Clay as Secretary of State. I think you will not be surprised to hear that the friends of Mr. Clay do not desire to separate West from West. (*Pauses to see if meaning is taken. Moves closer. They have stopped walking.*) Do I mistake in supposing your view of the matter to be not unlike mine, which is that in this Republic there are many able and ambitious men, among whom Mr. Clay might be included, who would not disgrace the first Cabinet post?

JACKSON: Our views of this matter have some correspondence, Mr. Búchanan. But speak on. Your preamble is not so little as was promised.

BUCHANAN: Senator Jackson, my question is merely this: have you ever intimated the intention ascribed to you, that is, to continue Mr. Adams as Secretary of State? If it could be contradicted, under your authority, by you expressly or by one of your confidential friends, that you have already selected your chief competitor for the highest office within your gift, then I have reason to believe that the Presidential contest can be settled within an hour.

JACKSON: I have not the least objection, Mr. Búchanan, to answering your question. I think well of Mr. Adams. He stood by me when the Indian-lovers would have had my hide for cleaning out the damnable Seminoles. But I have never intimated that I would, or would not, appoint him my Secretary of State. (*unleashing the fury of righteousness*) There are secrets I keep to myself. I will conceal them from the very hairs of my head! If I believed that my right hand knew what the left would do on the subject of appointments, I would cut it off and cast it into the fire! In politics as in all else my guide is principle alone. If I am elected President, it shall be without intrigue and solicitation. I shall enter office perfectly free and untrammeled, at perfect liberty to fill the offices of the government with the men I believe to be the ablest and best in the country!

BUCHANAN (*seeing how the game lies*): Your answer is such a one as I had expected to receive. I have not sought to obtain it for my own satisfaction; may I ask, am I at liberty to repeat your response to others?

JACKSON: Indeed you may, Mr. Búchanan. You may tell Mr. Clay and his friends that before I reach the Presidential chair by means of bargain and corruption I would see the earth open and swallow Mr. Clay and his friends and myself with them! Tell them, if they have not confidence in me to believe that if elected I will call to my aid in the Cabinet men of the first virtue, talent, and integrity—tell them not to vote for me!

BUCHANAN: I understand you, sir. I thank you for your patience. Good day; our day's duties await on Capitol Hill. (*He is anxious to leave;* JACKSON *stays him.*)

JACKSON: Between ourselves, Mr. Búchanan. (*draws closer, points to heart*) In here I carry Charles Dickinson's bullet, so close to my heart the surgeons feared to cut it out. I took his shot square in the chest and then I aimed. The villain couldn't believe his eyes; they had to hold him to the mark. He folded his arms across his chest so I shot him down below, in the parts of his manhood. He groaned for days before he died. More savages and villains have been dispatched at my command than could be housed in Gadsby's Hotel. (BUCHANAN *bows again but cannot leave.*) On my own hook, I should be dead ten times over. As a lad of thirteen I took my first wound; running messages for the Revolution, my brother Bob and me were caught. A swine of a British officer slashed his sabre at my skull—see this scar?—when I declined to clean the hogshit from his boots. Then they marched us forty miles to prison with open wounds. In the filth there we caught the smallpox. Then my sainted mother came and begged her boys' release and walked us home to the Waxhaws through a hurricane. My brother died of it. My other brother Hugh had already met his maker, courtesy of King George Three. Within the year another plague took off my mother; they tossed her body like a dog's into an unmarked grave, and sent me her clothes in a bundle. I have been alone ever since. When in Nashville it come into my head to take a horsewhip to the Benton brothers, one of their bullets broke my shoulder like a china cup; but I pulled a pistol on the doctor when the rogue unsheathed his knife to amputate. I crushed the British at New Orleans still bleeding from the wound; I routed the Creeks and

Seminoles so consumed with bowel complaint my fever fried the leather of the saddle. I've been there, Mr. Búchanan, and out the other side. You're still this side, and that makes a man gingerly. When I was a youngster in the Congress as you are now, I didn't go around tiptoeing on errands for the likes of Henry Clay; I stood right up on my own hind legs and in a big voice voted Nay to a farewell tribute for that sanctimonious old mule General George Washington. Soft on redcoats and redskins, he was, and I hated him for it. Young man, you mistake where the power in this country lies; it's not in the wits of the politicians, and never was in such a set of weasel holes. Mark my words: any bargain Clay and Adams work out between 'em'll be the ruin of 'em both. When ye've passed through to the other side, Mr. Búchanan, when ye've put the fear of the worst behind ye, ye'll know where the power lies in God's own country: it lies in the passions of the people. (*beats stomach*) With the people in yer guts, ye can do no wrong. Otherwise, wriggle as ye will, ye can do no right. Take your stand on principle, Mr. Búchanan, and never fear to make yourself enemies. (*walks away*)

BUCHANAN (*bowing after him*): I shall not, as long as you, General Jackson, never be counted among them.

*Enter* STEPHEN DOUGLAS—*a "steam engine in britches." As Murat Halstead saw him in 1860: ". . . a queer little man, leonine head and duck legs . . . The Little Giant wears his black hair long, but it is getting thin, and is not the great tangled mass we saw on his neck a few years ago. . . . His mouth is closed up as if he was trying to bite a pin in two. . . . He requires a large vest—and large as he is about the chest, his waist is becoming still more extensive. But he* has *an immense head—in height, and breadth and depth—in indications of solidity and force, you cannot find its equal in Washington." The time on the stage is December 3, 1857.* DOUGLAS *is played by the actor who played* ROBERT COLEMAN.

BUCHANAN: Mr. Douglas, how are we to allay the contention and trouble created by the strife over the Lecompton Constitution?

DOUGLAS: Why, Mr. President, I do not see how *you* should have any trouble in the premises. The Constitution says *Congress* shall make all needful rules and regulations respecting the Territories, but I cannot recall any clause which requires the President to make any.

BUCHANAN: Sir, since your Kansas-Nebraska Act reawakened chaos in the Territories, much is required of a President. It was a black day, Mr. Douglas, when upon your initiative the wise and tested safeguards of the Missouri Compromise were overthrown. The President is not among those who impugn your motives—who whisper that you abused your position as Chairman of the Committee on Territories to bring quick profit upon your holdings in Chicago real estate. But whatever the cause, the result is plain: a legal void having been created, settlers rush in from opposite sides and set about murdering one another. This is the Kansas your legislation has bequeathed to this administration.

DOUGLAS: The principle of squatter sovereignty—

BUCHANAN: The abstract principle, without the structure of implementation, does not exist. Rights are not bestowed by mere negation, but by a nurturing framework of constituted order. Where laws have not had time to take root, the bloodiest ruffians and most adroit fanatics will dominate. This is not democracy but its opposite, anarchy.

DOUGLAS: You trust mankind too little, and some men too

much. General Walker, whom you persuaded against his self-interest to be your Governor in Kansas, was betrayed, all Washington knows, by the Southern wing of your Cabinet while you were vacationing in Bedford.

BUCHANAN: The charge of betrayal, sir, can be carried lightly when it comes from all sides. So the fire-eaters accuse me of betraying the South, by begging the Kansans to redeem themselves with the ballot. Walker, an ambitious man, overstepped his commission; yet the President sustained his promises as party policy. I held out to the ten thousand voters of Kansas, four-fifths of them Freesoilers, the opportunity to vote for delegates to the constitutional convention, and in their abolitionist madness four-fifths of them refused to vote! What choice has the President, Mr. Douglas, but to uphold the legally constituted Lecompton government and to submit its application for Statehood to Congress? To do otherwise would pit the chief executive of this nation against the constituted legal authority of a locality, and make me as much a revolutionary as Jim Lane and the gunmen who pretend to rule Kansas from Topeka!

DOUGLAS: You are too close a lawyer not to admit that even your grounds of strict legality are dubious; for the Toombs enabling bill was defeated. In any case, fraud is rife. Only a fraction of those enfranchised voted, and those mostly dwell in Missouri; the South did not even send her responsible sons to fight this battle, but the most desperate of her riffraff. Mr. President, your course is plain: begin again, with popular submission. Discard both the Lecompton and Topeka constitutions, and either revert to the Toombs bill, upon which all Democrats agreed in the last session, or apply the Minnesota Enabling Act to Kansas.

BUCHANAN: Mr. Douglas, if I do that at the juncture we have

reached, I am assured that at least five southern States will proclaim secession. Please understand me. We seek the same end: an expanding, pacified Union. This Kansas agitation is an illusory crisis; all sides are agreed that slavery can never flourish on the dry plains of the West. Ratify Kansas as a State, and its voters will make short shrift of the peculiar institution, and the main cause of national exacerbation will be removed from celebrity. The peace of the entire Union is surely of more account than the temporary triumph of one or another faction on the edge of the wilderness.

DOUGLAS: You have never been west, I believe. A pity. You would have seen the future there.

BUCHANAN: I see future enough here in Washington to alarm me. The party, Mr. Douglas, that cannot unify behind their President on this issue will not unify to elect the next President; and if the next Chief Executive is to be a Black Republican, then I am the last President of the United States. Senator, for the sake of the Union, and the thirty millions of lives its sublime terrain nurtures, do not cross me in this. I am an old man. If I outlive my term, it will be God's will rather than my own. Your great days are yet to come.

DOUGLAS: The voters of Illinois would never return me to Congress, did I permit the principle of popular sovereignty to be so flagrantly mocked as it is by the drunken machinations of the sixty hacks, loafers, and Negro-traders who sit at Lecompton courtesy of the stuffed ballot-box!

BUCHANAN: The Convention has agreed to submit the question, with or without slavery, to a popular vote; your personal friend John Calhoun achieved this compromise against all odds, working closely with acting Governor Stanton, and our own special emissary Mr. Henry Martin.

Your Nebraska Act demands no more than this, that the Territory votes upon this one question of substance, with or without slavery.

DOUGLAS: Arsenic with or without butter is still arsenic. The Lecompton government exists as an arm of the continental slave power and all the nation north and south knows it. Mr. Calhoun, who has seen better days, may or may not have imagined he was implementing my will; but nothing will satisfy me, Mr. President, or the spirit of the Kansas-Nebraska Act, short of your fulfilling your promise, given explicitly in a letter to Walker before you betrayed him, for a full popular submission.

BUCHANAN: Such a submission will invite chaos to enter again, where the door is all but shut, and we need only turn the key in the lock. (*gestures imploringly*) You have been deaf, Mr. Douglas, to my attempt to explain my policy in terms of the vast exigencies that the President must necessarily consider. Let me then frame the matter more narrowly for you. Your hopes, which are great, lie within the Democratic party. And I have resolved to make Lecompton a test of party loyalty. Those in office who resist me will be decapitated. (*changes tone*) Between ourselves, Mr. Douglas. All is not as it might be in Kansas, but ours is a fallible world. Why deny the South this illusory aggrandizement, that will be swiftly wiped away by statehood itself, once attained? The United States have become, since the original loose union of seaboard farms, that thought alike and worked alike, a federation of differing halves; the one half, the North and its mills fed by the produce of the West, flourishes, while the other half languishes, infected by a corrupting and unprofitable institution. We who have health must keep this ailing partner within the house, and give her space and time to heal; lest in her fever she seek to escape, and burn down the house itself. My tongue tricks me into a telling gender; for so I put it to myself—the South is our wife, fair yet willful, delicate yet proud, who must be indulged in small things, that she may be transformed in the large.

DOUGLAS: Had you ever been a married man, Mr. President, you might adjust your metaphor; a firm rebuke, on the instant, harsh though it may appear, is a greater kindness to a wife, and more encourages her love, than a supine indulgence. With profound respect for your office, sir, I am honor-bound to resist you on Lecompton.

BUCHANAN: Mr. Senator, do you clearly apprehend the goal to which you are now tending?

DOUGLAS: Yes, sir; I have taken a through ticket, and checked all my baggage.

BUCHANAN: Mr. Douglas, I desire you to remember that no Democrat ever yet differed from an Administration of his own choice without being crushed. Beware of the fate of Tallmadge and Rives.

DOUGLAS: Mr. President, I wish *you* to remember that General Jackson is dead!

*Lights go out.* BUCHANAN *is alone, and repeats, puzzled:* Dead?

*Lights return slowly.*
*Enter* JAMES POLK: *"somber, stern, thin-lipped . . . a large, broad forehead, and he wore his hair combed straight back." He is another* JACKSON, *played by that same actor. The night of February 21, 1848.*

POLK: Not yet dead, Mr. Buchanan. But headed straight for the grave. Stricken by a paralytic affliction at his desk in the

House, and carried insensible from the Hall to the Speaker's Room.

BUCHANAN: I am sorry to learn of it, Mr. President. Though John Quincy Adams was never a political friend of mine, we have known each other in our public characters for two decades, and since joining your Cabinet I have had him for a neighbor on F Street. He possessed more wit than character, and more character than sense.

POLK: He was the last of the iron race that cut this continent loose from kingship. Politics ruined his administration, and ever after, politics has ruled the roost. It is a day for mourning, Mr. Buchanan, when public men cannot maintain a straight course. Since Jackson's great galleon passed, the sea is full of trimmers.

BUCHANAN: You speak with meaning, sir, but I doubt that I fathom it.

POLK: I allude, sir, to today's Cabinet meeting, and your extraordinary dissent from my decision to submit Trist's Mexican treaty to the Senate for ratification.

BUCHANAN: As your Secretary of State, I gave it as my true opinion that the treaty, which Trist has negotiated in defiance of his recall, should be rejected. I do not believe we should settle for anything less southerly than the line of the Sierra Madre.

POLK (*producing a ledger*): In August of 1845, Mr. Buchanan, principally in order to keep a record of your remarkable variations of opinion, I commenced to keep a diary of my days as President.

BUCHANAN (*bowing*): I am honored, Mr. President, to have been the prime motivator of a record that posterity, I am confident, will view as priceless.

POLK (*consulting*): Under the entry for May 13th, 1846, the

night that a state of war with Mexico was proclaimed, I find
you proposing that we declare to foreign governments our
intention to secure no territory south of the Del Norte;
that we did not wish to acquire either California or New
Mexico. At that time, my memory and my diary unite in
confirming, I overruled such a declaration as improper, expressing the opinion that territorial concessions might
prove to be Mexico's only means of indemnifying the claims
of our citizens upon her, and to defray the expense of the
war that her injuries and insolence had forced upon us.
*Now*, not two years later, you balk at the peace terms which
would give us all that you would have forehandedly dis-
avowed, protesting it is not enough!

BUCHANAN: Circumstances change, and so must opinions. Remember that I also opposed Scott's invasion of the interior.
But, now that Mexico City is occupied, and we have spent
so much of our treasure and our blood, the terms we ini-
tially held out become too lenient. Lord Palmerston is said
to have remarked in London, "They are going to take two-
thirds of Mexico? Why don't they take the whole?" There
exists a rising sentiment in the Democratic press for merci-
fully bringing the totality of this confused and incapable
land into the beneficial haven of our republican institutions.

POLK: Mr. Buchanan, I cannot help but labor under the conviction that the true reason of your present course is that
you are yourself a candidate for the Presidential nomination. In private, I am convinced, you approve of this treaty,
just as you did of the Oregon settlement, though once it
was assured you announced otherwise. You wish to throw
the full responsibility upon me. If the Mexican Treaty is
well received by the country, your aspirations will not be

injured; if, on the other hand, it is not received well, you can say, "I advised against it." No candidate for the Presidency ought to remain in the Cabinet. He is an unsafe adviser.

BUCHANAN: What is an adviser's duty, but to temper the necessary thrust of executive decision with a broader, more ambiguous view? One of my original reasons for reluctance in the Mexican venture was that the North, of its own sectional interest, would resist acquiring so much potential slave territory. The Wilmot Proviso has confirmed my anxieties. The storm in New England rages. Mr. President, have you sufficiently considered that, by enlarging the Union, you may break it in two?

POLK: New England, Mr. Buchanan, is no place to look for national policy. Adams is dying; he is their last voice of consequence. They may rant their sermons on the misery of the nigger, and a few retired men of means may spend a night in jail for refusing to pay their taxes, but since Massachusetts played the traitor's role in Madison's little war, and disgraced the Federalist party so it died of shame thereafter, this region is a thorn in our side merely. Howl though the Bostonians may, their descendants will not disdain to prosper in a nation squared off from coast to coast. To be President of the United States, sir, is to act as advocate for a blind, venomous, and ungrateful client; still, one must make the best of the case, for the purposes of Providence.

BUCHANAN: Not Boston alone, but New York and Philadelphia complain that their interests are brushed aside by a Southern Washington that pursues expansion too recklessly.

POLK: Not recklessly, reasonably. Upper California—unlike Chihuahua, and Sonora, and Cuba—is ours *de facto*; Mexico City is too distant and feeble to rule it, our American squatters already outnumber the Spanish-speaking of the region. I will settle for no less, and seek no more. (*draws closer*) Between ourselves, Mr. Buchanan. Your wavering courtship of public favor undoes your clear vision. You cannot be more martial than General Cass; you cannot outflank General Scott; if the nomination falls to them, then it must. Agile vacillation is no route to the Presidency: a firm course, rather, maintained with an inspired disregard of secondary effects.

BUCHANAN: Yet in matters of a continental scale, even secondary effects are life and death to many.

POLK (*drawing back*): I stand in no need of such preachments. Look at my hair, my hands. I entered this penitential office the youngest ever to occupy it, and will depart an old man. My insides have malfunctioned for four years in this choleric swamp. Officeseekers attack me like vermin; at night they emerge from the wainscoting. Nothing sustains me but consciousness of duty done: of a program projected and, with the ratification of this treaty, completed. I intend to submit it. Will you support me, or defy me?

BUCHANAN (*bowing*): Have I ever failed, though differing as your adviser, to carry out your will, in my capacity as functionary?

POLK: No. In your elusive fashion, you have shown loyalty. A Supreme Court seat would have been yours, had you been constant in wanting it. My opinion is, Mr. Buchanan, you would be happiest on the bench. But if your devil drives you to a more perilous height, go, and take my blessing. One word of practical advice: cease courting the Barnburners. You fundamentally err, in attempting to make friends of opponents. Any honest man has opponents; opposition demonstrates a steadfast direction. Learn to hate. The people love a good hater.

BUCHANAN: Poor Adams was a joyous hater, and his administration became a monument of futility. Now he lies dying.

POLK: Well, what is life for any of us, but a busy dying? Forgive me, I lack the time for philosophy. The Senate must have the treaty, ere the Mexicans change tyrants again, or Trist's incompetence is exposed. Purge yourself of ambiguity, my friend, and leave the Presidency to fate. *(Exit.)*

BUCHANAN *(alone)*: There is a profound wisdom in a remark of La Rochefoucauld with which I met the other day—"Les choses que nous désirons n'arrivent pas, ou, si elles arrivent, ce n'est, ni dans le temps, ni de la manière qui nous auraient fait le plus de plaisir."

HARRIET *(bustling through)*: Oh, Nunc, let's have my French lesson later; the company's about to arrive! Only Southerners and Secretary Black, nobody north of Philadelphia will come to the White House any more! I don't care, Mr. Seward and Douglas were so short I could never decide what lady to let them take in!

BUCHANAN: What is the menu?

HARRIET: It is *glo*rious. Oysters and terrapin from the Chesapeake, shad from the James, venison from Virginia, mutton from Vermont, and from Lancaster County, roast shoulder of pork, stuffed with sauerkraut and garnished with cinnamon apples! For dessert, your favorite, gooseberry tart, not to mention sweetmeats and syrupy wines imported from France and Spain, admitted under the low tariff the Southern Democrats wouldn't raise for you, after you broke your heart over Lecompton for *them*, and poor Aaron Brown died of the postal deficit! To end up, for those still awake, port and brandy, chartreuse and crème de cacao, and

English mints just like we used to buy on Marylebone
Road!

BUCHANAN: Banquet enough, for the edge of an abyss.

HARRIET: Nunc, you're such a dull stick lately. You've been
wanting to meet Mrs. Keitt for months; Mr. Slidell *promises* she's the loveliest woman in Washington!

BUCHANAN (*slyly*): And is it true, dear Harriet, that our fire-
eating Congressman turned to the courtship of Susanna
Sparks only after you, "The Great Mother of the Indians,"
had repelled as fiercely as a squaw his incendiary advances?

HARRIET: Now, Nunc: nosy is as nosy does. I'm all of twenty-
seven, and full-blown as I'll ever be. A girl must have her
secrets.

BUCHANAN: And is it true, as my scandalized servants report,
that you communicate with Sophie Plitt by means of a
locked butter kettle? On my honor I swear, I opened your
previous letters by mistake, and glanced at them solely for
evidence of treason.

HARRIET (*shakes finger*): You were a silly wicked uncle to do
that. As La Rochefoucauld says, "Notre défiance justifie la
tromperie d'autrui."

BUCHANAN: But also he says, "L'usage ordinaire de la finesse
est la marque d'un petit esprit."

HARRIET: L'esprit!—"L'esprit est toujours la dupe du cœur."

*Enter* HOWELL COBB—*plump, quick, rich, Georgian, forty-five—
and* MRS. COBB, *née Lamar. Same actors as* SLAYMAKER *and* GRACE
HUBLEY. *Decided Southern accents.* MRS. COBB *is very pregnant.*

COBB: What's all this frog-talk I hear about finesse? You must
be talking about our finesseful Old Squire, right, Miss
Lane? You *do* look ravishing. (*kisses her on the cheek*)

MRS. COBB: Oh, Mr. President, I'm so *sorry* about our unspeak-

able opponents winning Governor in Pennsylvania. Howell said to me, "Mary," he said, "Armageddon is here," but
I said to him, "Think of poor Mr. Buchanan, how badly he
must feel *personally*!" (*kisses him on cheek*)

BUCHANAN: My native commonwealth has ever been an un-
ruly student of party regularity, Mrs. Cobb. Informants
write me that she is thoroughly free-soiled and abolition-
ized, and the tariff is not the entire cause. Even the moun-
taineers betrayed the party of Jackson. Nevertheless,
Madame, let us not altogether abandon hope. The national
elections are two weeks off; a fusion ticket might yet save
the Keystone State for Breckinridge.

COBB: The Douglas committee has agreed to withdraw, but
your old friend Forney and his Philadelphia clique continue to keep the Douglas slate on the ballot—some say the
split is designed as a present to the Black Republicans,
whom Forney is about to join.

BUCHANAN: Poor Forney. All his devotion turned to spite. And
what of fusion in New York?

COBB: *Con*fusion is more the word. The Breckinridge Volunteers demanded the lieutenant-governorship, the canal
commissioner, and ten electors. The Douglasites refused to
go higher than six electors, even though the downtown
merchants, with visions of millions in cotton credits going
up in smoke, had pledged two hundred thousand dollars to
a united ticket. The state committee empowered Rich-
mond and Cagger to keep trading; they went and drew the
Bell men in and arrived at an electoral ticket of eighteen
Douglas, ten Bell, and seven Breckinridge. The torchlit
ratification rally at Cooper Union was just gorgeous,
Squire, just gorgeous; but the inside money predicts a Republican majority of at least fifty thousand. Seymour of
Connecticut assured me in confidence that Tammany's true

objective is to get Schnell out of the customhouse, which would be best achieved by the election of (*looks around gleefully*)—Ape Lincoln!

BUCHANAN: Ach, the muddle. All this parochial greed, while the temple trembles. The conservative mass, north and south, want peace!

COBB (*taken aback*): Why, so do we all, Mr. President.

*Enter* JOHN BUCHANAN FLOYD—*outwardly impressive, inwardly distraught; Virginian, fifty-four—and* MRS. FLOYD. *Same actors as* REYNOLDS *and* MRS. JENKINS.

FLOYD: Peace within the Union, or without it, Mr. Cobb?

COBB: Why, wherever it may be found, Mr. Floyd.

FLOYD: I do not think it a smiling matter. Virginia has supplied seven Presidents to the White House; Georgia, not one. Secession, sir, is a fighting word in the western part of my State.

COBB: Governor Floyd, let us speak honestly, as is the custom among gentlemen. While you as it were inherited the governorship as a legacy from your esteemed father, I won Georgia from the grip of secessionists, by allying myself with Union Whigs. Ask any Yankee which Southerner speaks most fervently and frequently for the sacred Union; the answer will be my name, unless it be the name of my fellow Georgian Alexander Stephens. In a time of much public asperity, and of many rumored scandals, not one congressional voice has ever impugned my management of the national Treasury. My love for the Union, sir, is written in ink and proven in iron.

FLOYD (*to him alone, as* BUCHANAN *is engaged by the ladies*): Judas! All Washington knows you connive with Thompson and Toombs daily, to put yourself in the forefront of secession!

COBB (*privately*): My State leads, but yours must follow, Mr. Floyd. The die is cast, and has been long cast. But we must humor old Buck a few more months, lest he put obstacles in the way of an amiable departure.

FLOYD: I have no use for duplicity, sir.

COBB: Then you are as poor a man for politics as you are for business. John, you can ill afford delicate scruples; every day, some new stench arises from the War Department. (*He has indignantly lifted his voice, so that* BUCHANAN *overhears. The Old Chief joins them.*)

BUCHANAN: I overheard a fragment, and must agree, Mr. Floyd. Howell, as ever, is right. You have sold cheap and bought dear whenever such opportunity arose. You have permitted friend and foe alike to abuse your trusting nature. By what law, I ask, did you sign acceptances on those Russell, Majors, and Waddell bills?

FLOYD: There was no law, Mr. President, but the procedure has always been used in emergencies.

BUCHANAN: Well, if there is no law for it, it is against the law.

FLOYD: The fault lay with Congress, for not appropriating the money needed to send our expedition against the Mormons. Sir, I accept your admonition, and I am resigned that the Republican press and the Congress harry me without respite; but I resent suffering insult and reproval from a fellow Cabinet member.

COBB: What he means, Squire, is we Southerners better stick together.

BUCHANAN: Yes, let's save our ammunition for the enemy.

SOUTHERNERS *laugh, too uproariously.*

MRS. FLOYD (*to cover up*): One rainbow, surely, Mr. President, is the way that monster Douglas is exterminatin' himself with every silly speech he makes! Why, he runs around down South spoutin' like he thought he could make the Mississippi flow backwards into Illinois!

MRS. COBB: They say he travels in fear of his train being wrecked and a tar-and-feather party materializing on the spot!

HARRIET: If there is such a party, Adele Douglas will no doubt congratulate herself that we of the White House were excluded from the guest list. (*laughter*)

COBB: Indeed, Squire, Douglas is crushed as thoroughly as you ever desired. Though he shout himself hoarse for Union, the Pennsylvania results have stampeded Southern voters toward Breckinridge. In Montgomery, the Little Giant was pelted with rotten eggs. Those who have seen him say there is death in his face.

FLOYD: Yet, I understand that in Nashville he outdrew Yancey. In Chattanooga also he attracted great crowds, and in Atlanta. The mass of average men cling to him as the one spar in a shipwreck, the one voice willing to cry down both abolition and secession.

BUCHANAN: It does grieve me, that Douglas and I came to such enmity. I had hoped to be reconciled, for all his coarse railling. There was little between us save this phantom question of the Territories. Had he, at Charleston, accepted the platform he accepted at Baltimore, the very platform I had advocated, a mere acknowledgment of the Supreme Court's right of jurisdiction over property, then we might now be a united party headed for victory, and the nation headed for safe haven. I wonder, in my personal intercourse with Douglas, if my own better nature was not betrayed, by a possibly unwarranted impatience.

COBB: *Well* warranted, sir. Stephen A. Douglas is the epitome of heedless opportunism and spendthrift folly.

BUCHANAN: His effort to hold the South from panic, when he has no hope of victory, shows something magnanimous. It plagues my conscience, Howell, that we harried him too hard over Lecompton.

COBB: What we did to Douglas, we did for party discipline, to rebuff anarchy. By way of thanks we were treated to the infamous and unconstitutional Covode Investigation, whose big black book of a so-called report now circulates everywhere, to the jubilation of Lincolnite and Douglasite alike.

BUCHANAN: Indeed, the precedent is dangerous.

COBB: Ever since his Nebraska Act destroyed all safeguards this man Douglas has disrupted the national order for his own publicity; you have been lenient and forbearing to a saintly degree; waste no remorse upon him. He scorned your temperance; now let him choke on bombast and booze. You would stoop to those who have vowed to destroy you, when you stand immune upon the high ground of principle.

BUCHANAN: But must I not be guided, in my office, by the supreme principle of national well-being? In my sleep the people cry for peace. With our support, and Bell's withdrawal, Douglas might carry the border states, and then, in New Jersey—

LAWRENCE KEITT *and his wife* SUSANNA *enter. She is played by the actress who played* ANNE COLEMAN.

KEITT: Sooner fire consort with water than the pure spirit of the South tolerate a minion of those Northern bankers who sent John Brown south to drench our land in blood! Breckinridge or the Devil! The North is a Moloch, gentlemen; it fattens on our cotton, enchains us in debt, denies us the West, pollutes our heritage with mongrel immigrants, and presently will postulate that our wives and infants submit to a baboon reign of black savagery! May Douglas roast with Sumner and Wendell Phillips, for all his doughface platitudes; I say, and say it openly, break the grip of this evil vampire of the North, and create, with Cuba, a free paradise based upon the divinely ordained institution of African slavery!

COBB *takes* KEITT *aside*. BUCHANAN *walks toward* SUSANNA. FLOYD *intrudes*.

FLOYD: Mr. President, may I have an urgent word with you?

BUCHANAN: Mr. Floyd, I am out of patience with your explanations. This affair with Captain Meigs has vexed me greatly. For the sake of harmony and appearances I have agreed to transfer him to the Dry Tortugas, against my better judgment; since in his quarrels with you I know him to have been unfailingly on the side of what is scrupulous and strict. On top of this I was astonished to learn, sir, that you have let the contract for heating the Capitol building to a passel of Virginians who scarcely know a furnace from a flue. We will speak of these sorry matters later. Please, allow me to greet this good lady.

FLOYD *turns angrily away, and joins* COBB *and* KEITT.

BUCHANAN: Madame, my ears have long been caressed by the rumor that your beauty is without peer in Washington City. Now it gratifies my eyes to be witness to this truth. Welcome to this house, in a troubled time.

SUSANNA: Oh, Mr. President sir, it's so terrifying now, everybody up in arms, and talking about *war*, and having duels right on the floor of the Congress! And just the way the darkies look at you on the street here is so different from how they do back home in Charleston!

BUCHANAN: Alas, our dusky brethren have been stirred to false hopes and vain aspirations by the delirious pamphlets of the abolitionists and by the freesoil rhetoric heard whenever Congress sits in session. Nothing grieves the President more, in these dark days, than that angelic Southern matrons must retire each night a-tremble for the safety of their children. Yet I would beg you, pity the black man in his impudent delusions, for the sudden suspension of the institution that enfolds him would do no race greater harm than his own.

SUSANNA: Lawrence says, soon as Lincoln and his rascals get themselves elected, the blacks will rise up in a foaming tide of murder, rape, and pillage!

BUCHANAN: My dear Mrs. Keitt, with all my heart I beg you to resist unreasoning panic. Republicans as well as Northern Democrats deplored John Brown's insane venture. The Negroes themselves were unmoved by it. My own effort will be, in the treacherous months ahead, to emphasize, for benefit of the South, the iron constraints with which the Constitution has wisely ringed the power of the Presidency. With Congress against him, Lincoln is paralyzed. Even with a Republican Congress, which is impossible—for this October's elections, amid many disappointments, showed a net gain of five Democratic seats—even *with* Congress, the President cannot alter the smallest detail of domestic institutions within a State. Sumner himself admits as much.

SUSANNA (*theatrically, for the benefit as well of the other ladies*): I do swear, rather than live in Niggerdom I would perish by my own hand!

BUCHANAN (*genuinely alarmed*): Dear lady, say not so! The thought alone is blasphemy.

MRS. COBB: My goodness, Mrs. Keitt, you do take on excessively! *My* husband assures me there will be no violence whatsoever. If Howell has said to me once, he has said a thousand times, it would save him a *for*tune to free his slaves, but he knows they'd starve and die naked without him. He loves them just like children and, what's more, Mrs. Keitt, they love him. In Georgia we're not afraid of our pickaninnies.

MRS. FLOYD: Mr. Buchanan, I've never been able to guess, what you exactly think, of our peculiar institution.

BUCHANAN: Why, I've proclaimed my opinion often; publicly, just last July, from the White House portico itself, to the body of a Breckinridge rally. (*goes to podium*) What would I, as a Pennsylvanian, say or do, supposing anybody was to contend that the legislature of any Territory could outlaw iron or coal within that Territory? The principle is precisely the same. The Supreme Court of the United States have decided—what was known to us all to have been the existing state of affairs for fifty years—that slaves are property. Admit that fact, and you admit everything. (*cheers*)

SUSANNA: Oh, Mr. Buchanan, can it be true, Lincoln is sure to triumph? Have we no hope?

HARRIET (*to her*): I have often heard Mr. Buchanan express the conviction that, were Douglas, Breckinridge, and Bell all to withdraw, a compromise candidate satisfactory to every Democrat would sweep the South, the border states, Pennsylvania, New York, and Indiana!

SUSANNA: But who could such a candidate be?

HARRIET: He would have to be a man of the North, but a proven friend of the South; a legalist able irrefutably to define the right, yet a passionate lover of peace; an official of broad experience foreign and domestic, yet a rigorous party regular; a man rich in years and wisdom, yet with a child's affirmative spirit.

SUSANNA: This is no man you describe, but a Savior!

BUCHANAN (*still at podium, raised above them*): There are in our midst numerous persons who predict the dissolution of the great Democratic party, and others who contend that it has already been dissolved. The wish is father to the thought. It has been heretofore in great peril; but when divided for the moment, it has always closed up its ranks and become more powerful, even from defeat. It will never die whilst the Constitution and the Union survive. It will live to protect and defend both. It has its roots in the very vitals of the Constitution, and, like one of the ancient cedars of Lebanon, it will flourish to afford shelter and protection to that sacred instrument, and to shield it against every storm of faction. (*Cheering from the machine at the back of the theatre. The ladies applaud.*)

SUSANNA *cries:* Oh, Mr. Buchanan, it's going to be *you!*

COBB (*in his group*): Hear that, gentlemen! Old Pub Func wants to run again!

FLOYD: The appetite of a python sits light, compared to the power-lust of these antique officeholders! Their jaws forget how to close. Dying before our eyes, battered and ridiculed as no President before him, still he maneuvers to prolong the torment. Disgusting!

KEITT: Never trust a doughface. They'll gobble their fill from the southern side of the feed trough; then squeal like pigs at the sticking point.

COBB: Never fear, in the end Old Buck always goes along with the Administration. (*male laughter*)

MRS. FLOYD: Oh, Mr. President, if only we could crown you King!

BUCHANAN: The Constitution, I fear, explicitly forbids it.

MRS. COBB: But we all know, there will *never* be war as long as you occupy the White House. Look at the wonderful way you bullied Brigham Young. Look at how you sent the Navy into Paraguay, where they don't even have an ocean!

BUCHANAN (*to* SUSANNA): Even you feel it, my dear, young as you are? The abyss at our feet?

SUSANNA: Yes! My husband is determined to die. Save us!

WOMEN *cry:* Save us, save us! MEN *laugh.* BUCHANAN *yearns from the podium, mouth ajar, held frozen as if in crystal.*

SUSANNA: (*curiously, after reaching out to him in a gesture reminiscent of* ANNE *in the woods*): I think he is impotent. I fear he does not love me, much as he protests he does.

KEITT: Come away, my firefly. In a little while, this nightmare will pass, and I shall be Governor of South Carolina, and Charleston the peer of Paris, and the Sultan of Turkey will send us perfumed emissaries.

FLOYD: You ladies also. A dead rattler still spouts poison. (*to* COBB, *the ladies and* KEITT *having left the stage*) I distrust this revolution. It is the child of the same stiffness that has embarrassed me in the Senate; Jefferson Davis is my persecutor.

COBB: You are Secretary of War; inefficiency and delay are now the first works of your department. Our Army is happily scattered across the West; the coastal forts are defended by a handful. Let matters thus remain, and your duty to yourself and the South is performed.

FLOYD: You speak airily; but blood runs through this.

COBB: Force nothing. Events will unfold of their own.

SUSANNA *runs onto stage, the front of her dress torn. She cries:* The beast! The beast has been elected! (*to* BUCHANAN) Laugh, Jim. Rage. Assault me. Anything but this regretful gazing.

*No response. She runs from stage, out other side. Stage darkens, but for spotlight on* BUCHANAN. *He slowly unfreezes, begins to read.*

BUCHANAN: In order to justify a resort to revolutionary resistance the federal government must be guilty of "a deliberate, palpable, and dangerous exercise" of powers not granted by the Constitution. The late Presidential election, however, has been held in strict conformity with its express provisions. How, then, can the result justify a revolution to destroy this very Constitution? Reason, justice, a regard for the Constitution, all require that we shall wait for some overt and dangerous act on the part of the President-elect, before resorting to such a remedy. It is said, however, that the antecedents of the President-elect have been sufficient to justify the fears of the South that he will attempt to invade their constitutional rights. But are such apprehensions of contingent danger in the future sufficient to justify the immediate destruction of the noblest system of government ever devised by mortals? This government is a great and powerful government, invested with all the attributes of sovereignty over the special subjects to which its authority extends. Its framers never intended to implant in its bosom the seeds of its own destruction, nor were they at its creation guilty of the absurdity of providing for its own dissolution. It was not intended by its framers to be the baseless fabric of a vision, which, at the touch of the enchanter, would vanish into thin air, but a substantial and mighty fabric, capable of resisting the slow decay of time, and of defying the storms of ages. In short, let us look the danger fairly in the face: secession is neither more nor less than revolution. It may or may not be a justifiable revolution; but still it is revolution.

What, in the meantime, is the responsibility and true position of the Executive? He is bound by solemn oath, before God and the country, "to take care that the laws be faithfully executed," and from this obligation he cannot be absolved by any human power. But what if the performance of this duty, in whole or in part, has been rendered impracticable by events over which he could have exercised no control? Such, at the present moment, is the case throughout the State of South Carolina. All the federal officers within its limits have already resigned. We no longer have a district judge, a district attorney, or a marshal in South Carolina. In regard to the property of the United States in South Carolina: this has been purchased for a fair equivalent, "by the consent of the legislature of the State," "for the erection of forts, magazines, arsenals," &c., and over these the authority "to exercise exclusive legislation" has been expressly granted by the Constitution to Congress. It is not believed that any attempt will be made to expel the United States from this property by force; but if in this I should prove to be mistaken, the officer in command of the forts has received orders to act strictly on the defensive. In such a contingency the responsibility for consequences would rightfully rest upon the heads of the assailants.

Apart from the execution of the laws, so far as this may be practicable, the Executive has no authority to decide what shall be the relations between the federal government and South Carolina. He has been invested with no such discretion. He possesses no power to change the relations heretofore existing between them, much less to acknowledge the independence of that State. It is, therefore, my duty to submit to Congress the whole question in all its bearings. The question fairly stated is: Has the Constitution delegated to Congress the power to coerce a State into submission? After much serious reflection, I have arrived at the conclusion that no such power has been delegated to Congress or to any other department of the federal government. The fact is, that our Union rests upon public opinion, and can never be cemented by the blood of its citizens shed in civil war. If it cannot live in the affections of the people it must one day perish. Congress possesses many means of preserving it by conciliation; but the sword was not placed in their hand to preserve it by force.

But may I be permitted solemnly to invoke my countrymen to pause and deliberate, before they determine to destroy this, the grandest temple which has ever been dedicated to human freedom since the world began. It has been consecrated by the blood of our fathers, by the glories of the past, and by the hopes of the future. The Union has already made us the most prosperous, and ere long will, if preserved, render us the most powerful nation on the face of the earth. In every foreign region of the globe the title of American citizen is held in the highest respect, and when pronounced in a foreign land it causes the hearts of our countrymen to swell with honest pride. Surely, when we reach the brink of the yawning abyss we shall recoil with horror from the last fatal plunge. (*Steps down, weary. No applause.*)

BUCHANAN (*to* FLOYD): Have the forts in Charleston harbor been reinforced? If those forts should be taken by South Carolina in consequence of our neglect to put them in defensible condition, it were better for you and me both to be thrown into the Potomac with millstones tied about our necks.

FLOYD: Sir, I will risk my honor and my life that South Carolina will not molest the forts.

BUCHANAN: That is all very well. But does that secure the forts?

FLOYD: Governor Gist, advised of the conciliatory logic of your message to Congress, has sent messages assuring us that, until the ordinance of secession is passed, everything is quiet and will remain so, if no more soldiers or munitions are sent on.

BUCHANAN: And what do we hear from Major Anderson?

FLOYD: He has taken undue alarm from the drilling of State troops in the streets of Charleston, amid public boasting of the intent to take Fort Moultrie. He prepared a requisition to draw one hundred muskets from the Charleston arsenal. Colonel Huger at the arsenal has asked the War Department for orders. I have informed him that authority to supply arms to the forts would be deferred for the present. I have replied to Major Anderson that any increase in the force under his command would add to the local excitement and might lead to serious results.

*Enter the members of the South Carolina congressional delegation*—KEITT, WILLIAM PORCHER MILES, JOHN MC QUEEN, M. L. BONHAM, W. W. BOYCE. (*These same actors subsequently take the parts of the Carolina "Commissioners," Senator* DAVIS, *and Secretary of Interior* THOMPSON.)

KEITT: Sir: we are here as Congressmen from the sovereign State of South Carolina. In less than two weeks we expect that secession will be proclaimed in Charleston. When this occurs, we will send commissioners to treat with you over the future relations between our two independent republics.

MILES (*more conciliatory*): In the meantime, Mr. President, we desire to reach some agreement with you that will prevent bloodshed.

BUCHANAN: Gentlemen, put whatever you wish to recommend in writing. But I am bitterly grieved at this disposition to desert the Union before you have been in any particular injured.

KEITT: Tell us this, then: do you intend, grieved or no, to use force in collecting federal revenues in Charleston harbor?

BUCHANAN (*stung by his tone*): I will obey the laws. I am no warrior—I am a man of peace—but I will obey the laws.

CONGRESSMEN, *exchanging looks and murmurs, leave.*

BUCHANAN (*to* FLOYD *and* COBB): Their taste is for fire, let them eat hearty of it. South Carolina has indulged herself in defiance before, and been isolated. What happens in Charleston harbor little matters if Georgia holds firm—is that not so, my dear Howell?

COBB: Mr. President, you know with what devotion I have furthered your advancement, and advised your administration.

BUCHANAN: And you know, Mr. Cobb, with how much affection I have received your support, and enjoyed your company. Though I have been honored with an acquaintanceship as wide as half the world, intimacy has been a rarity in my life, and I have perhaps too heavily leaned upon your friendship; my spies tell me that Mrs. Cobb has often complained of the long hours during which the President demanded your attendance.

COBB: Mrs. Cobb knew that by serving you I was serving the nation, and with the nation our children's future. However, times are sadly changed. Mrs. Cobb has returned to Georgia to await her confinement. My entire family there has mounted the blue cockade. My brother Thomas gives secessionist speeches that last for five hard-breathing hours, and my uncle John proclaims that "resistance to oppression is obedience to God." (*tries one more joke*) Squire, you know kin, they're as hard to herd as chickens in a whirlwind. (BUCHANAN *is not amused.* COBB *continues grimly.*) I had hoped to persuade the people of Georgia to remain in the Union until March 4th, so that I could man my post in your Cabinet to the end. But—

BUCHANAN: But, Howell, opportunity calls, in the perfidious new nation that is creating, and your financial embarrassments have been mysteriously eased by a spate of philanthropy from your disunionist brother-in-law.

COBB: Sir, let me finish. I have long proclaimed you to be "the truest friend to the South that ever sat in the Presidential chair." But as you dealt with these gentlemen from South Carolina, and refused them satisfaction, I saw that you and I have parted in policy, and so must part in fact.

BUCHANAN: Go, then, Cobb. I cannot bless your departure; nor can I prevent it.

COBB: A word more. Secretary Black—

BUCHANAN: No more words. I deeply trusted you. We shall not speak again. (*sits at desk, weaker*)

*The South Carolina* CONGRESSMEN *return, with a piece of paper.*

BONHAM: Our written statement, sir.

BUCHANAN (*reading it*): I do not like the word "provided." South Carolina will not molest Moultrie and Sumter, "provided that no reinforcements shall be sent into those forts, and their relative military status shall remain as at present." I cannot restrict my freedom with any guarantees. Further, your delegation has no official status and cannot bind anyone to its terms.

BOYCE: By relative military status, we mean that the transfer of the Moultrie garrison to Fort Sumter would be the equivalent of a reinforcement and justify an attack.

BUCHANAN (*thinking hard*): Though I can pledge you nothing, I can state to you that it is my policy not to alter the status quo.

MC QUEEN: May we have that in writing, Mr. President?

BUCHANAN (*equivocating*): After all, this is a matter of honor among gentlemen. I do not know that any paper or writing is necessary. We understand each other.

KEITT: I doubt that we do. How shall we know if you change your mind, and send troops after all?

BUCHANAN (*smiling*): Then I would first return this paper.

*They leave;* BUCHANAN *bows his head as if to pray; but* SLIDELL *enters.*

SLIDELL: Buchanan, I am astounded to be told that you refused the South Carolina delegation a simple promise not to reinforce the forts, after they had extended to you any number of manly and generous assurances!

BUCHANAN: Which they had no authority to extend. And they asked, Senator, for what the President cannot give.

SLIDELL: Your hand is weak, and growing weaker. Georgia is

going, and the Gulf States cannot stay. Why stick at these forts, when a continent teeters?

BUCHANAN: Sadly, Senator, do I perceive that you, too, would tip us toward disunion. That Keitt, and Rhett, and Yancey and other discontented small fry seek to manufacture opportunities within upheaval I can comprehend; but that you, and Toombs, and Davis, who have held sway over Washington— No, I can no longer give ear to your advice, and regret that I heeded it so long.

SLIDELL: That advice made you President.

BUCHANAN: And would unmake me now.

SLIDELL: Buchanan, don't be an imbecile. Your interest has always lain South, and still lies there.

BUCHANAN: *Mr.* James Buchanan, as a seeker of his own interest, is dead. There remains only the President of the United States. He has many duties to perform. Sir, you are excused. (SLIDELL *storms out.* BUCHANAN *yearns after. A moment of total darkness possesses the stage.*)

Enter JEREMIAH BLACK—*a harshly masculine man, big-boned, shaggy-browed; ornate and avid in thought; a fanatic legalist, anti-Republican, and Campbellite. Played by the actor who played* EDWARD BUCHANAN.

BLACK: General Cass has resigned, because you will not reinforce the forts. Here is his letter.

BUCHANAN (*reading, laughs*): Where was this fine bravado when he sat in Cabinet dozing off beneath his wig? I have often had occasion to remember what General Jackson said to me of Cass, when he sent him to Paris; he said, "Cass decides nothing for himself, but comes to me constantly with great bundles of paper." Well, Black, we'll no longer have to write his dispatches for him.

BLACK: I understand he already regrets his resignation, and would like it retracted.

BUCHANAN: Indeed? Quickly then, write me a letter of acceptance full of courteous and patriotic flowers. I have a new Secretary of State: you, Mr. Black.

BLACK: Mr. President, you honor me. For my replacement as Attorney-General, let me recommend my assistant, Edwin M. Stanton of Pittsburgh. He is incomparably informed upon the great land cases presently coming before the Supreme Court, and in my estimation all the land between the oceans does not harbor a more brilliant lawyer.

BUCHANAN: He is not well versed, I believe, in constitutional theory. And I have it from many sides that Stanton is not to be trusted.

BLACK: An unlooked-for stricture, Mr. President, from one who so long trusted Howell Cobb, and who still trusts John Floyd.

BUCHANAN: Floyd is a muddler, perhaps, but not a villain.

BLACK: In the capacity of Secretary of War, it is villainous to muddle as Floyd has done.

BUCHANAN (*waves wearily*): Very well, Stanton is our man. My heart is not in this, Black. A fight beckons, when all my being strains to mourn, and to mingle its dread with the dust.

*Exit* BLACK.
*Enter* KEITT *and* ANNE COLEMAN *together.*

KEITT: The union now subsisting between South Carolina and the other States, under the name of the United States of America, is hereby dissolved.

ANNE: Come away with me, Jim. When I died, I made a miraculous discovery; there is no abyss. The abyss is only the height of our fear, seen in a mirror. When I took opium, my father ceased to thunder, my heart ceased to batter at the motionless image of you.

KEITT: Governor Pickens demands that you yield possession of Fort Moultrie immediately.

BUCHANAN (*to* ANNE): And did you die to do me spite? Could you be such a traitor to our love?

ANNE: Ere your love proved traitor to me. (*recites*)

> "For the sword outwears its sheath,
>     And the soul wears out the breast,
> And the heart must pause to breathe,
>     And Love itself have rest."

Late that November I saw life to be of a desperate impurity. You could have followed, had you loved, but your evil God bid you live, live and breathe and scheme. Every minute of your life, Jim, has affronted our love. Now look; you are an old man. Fifty years of deceit have worn thin as a coat of lime, and all our nation proclaims your treachery.

*Moment of darkness.*

JEFFERSON DAVIS *enters, with other Southerners—R. M. T. Hunter and W. H. Trescot (silent parts). It is the morning of December 27th, 1860.*

DAVIS: Have you received any intelligence from Charleston in the last three hours?

BUCHANAN: No.

DAVIS: Then I have a great calamity to announce to you. Major Anderson, during the night last night, under cover of darkness, spiked the guns at Fort Moultrie and moved his full force to Fort Sumter. Now, Mr. President, you are surrounded with blood and dishonor on all sides.

BUCHANAN (*rising from his desk, leaning against the mantel, crushing a cigar in the palm of his hand*): My God, are calamities never to come singly? I call God to witness—you gentlemen better than anybody *know*—that this is not only without but *against* my orders. It is against my policy.

DAVIS: Then swiftly, sir, condemn Anderson's action and order him back to Moultrie; reprisals from South Carolina may yet be avoided. The certain alternative is war.

BUCHANAN: But I cannot condemn Major Anderson without the facts. I must call a Cabinet meeting. Trust me, gentlemen, trust me. If our gentlemen's agreement has indeed been broken, it will be repaired.

SOUTHERNERS *leave. Cabinet*—FLOYD, BLACK, STANTON, THOMPSON—*storms in. (Silent parts for Isaac Toucey, Joseph Holt, Philip Thomas)*

FLOYD: Anderson has betrayed us all. He has compromised the President, and made war inevitable! This catastrophic maneuver was totally against his orders.

BLACK: On the contrary, sir, it was in precise accordance with his orders.

FLOYD: Mr. Black, it was not. It could not have been.

BLACK: Mr. Floyd, I have sent to the War Department for these orders of December 11th, drawn up by Major Anderson and Major Buell, and endorsed by you. I shall read. "The smallness of your force will not permit you, perhaps, to occupy more than one of the three forts, but an attack or an attempt to take possession of any of them will be regarded as an act of hostility, and you may then put your command into either of them which you may deem most proper, to increase its power of resistance. You are also authorized to take similar steps whenever you have tangible evidence of a design to proceed to a hostile act."

FLOYD: Indeed so; I defy you to produce "tangible evidence of a design to proceed to a hostile act."

STANTON (*short and pugnacious; the actor who played* DOUGLAS *and* ROBERT COLEMAN, *but wearing Stanton's well-known wire-rim spectacles and his rather Pharaonic beard*): Sir, a resolution has been publicly introduced into the South Carolina legislature for possession of all the forts! The Charleston *Mercury* insists on it daily! The very workmen employed at Fort Sumter openly sport the blue cockade!

FLOYD: Rumors and gestures, merely; not justification for a defiant military action. Anderson left the guns at Moultrie spiked and burnt the carriages; such warlike tactics utterly violate the solemn pledge given by this government.

STANTON: When was any such pledge given? Where does it exist in writing?

BLACK: Mr. Floyd, you are impugning the honor of the President of the United States.

BUCHANAN (*as if awakened*): I promised nothing certain. I agree that Major Anderson's maneuver, though unexpected, was justified by the discretion granted him in explicit orders.

FLOYD (*grandly*): Then, if orders from the War Department are to replace honor among men, one remedy alone is left, and that is to withdraw the garrison from Charleston harbor altogether! I demand the right to order withdrawal.

BLACK (*brandishing papers*): Mr. Floyd, there never was a moment in the history of England when a minister of the Crown could have proposed to surrender a military post which might be defended, without bringing his head to the block!

STANTON: Such a surrender would be a crime like Arnold's, and all the participants should be hanged like André; the President who would issue such an order would be guilty of treason!

BUCHANAN: Oh, no! Not so bad as that, my friend—not so bad as that!

JACOB THOMPSON (*pale, stocky, played by the actor who played* BOYCE): Mr. President. South Carolina is a tiny State, with a sparse white population. The United States is a powerful nation with a vigorous government. This great nation can well afford to say to South Carolina, "See, we will withdraw our garrison as an evidence that we mean you no harm."

STANTON: Mr. President: the proposal to be generous implies that the government is strong, and that we, as the public servants, have the confidence of the people. I think that is a mistake. No administration has ever suffered the loss of public confidence and support as this has done. Only the other day it was announced that millions of dollars had been stolen from Mr. Thompson's department. The bonds were found to have been taken from the vault where they should have been kept, and the notes of Mr. Floyd were substituted for them. Now it is proposed to give up Sumter. All I have to say is that no administration, much less this one, can afford to lose a million of money and a fort in the same week!

FLOYD: Mr. President, this attorney has shared our counsels a few days and he presumes to sit in judgment upon those of us loyal to you and this administration for four years! The truth of the matter of these acceptances is that, had I not signed them, our troops, through the negligence of Congress, would have been left unequipped in the wilderness of Utah! Not a dollar has been lost to the government through my department; the malfeasances of the Yankee contractor

Russell and Mr. Thompson's appointee Bailey leave my honor untouched.

THOMPSON: Mr. President, I did not sleep for three nights, unravelling this monstrous theft from the safe of the Indian Trust Fund. Mr. Floyd's friends and kin are palpably incriminated; I intend to see *all* involved prosecuted to the limit of the law.

FLOYD: Mr. President, to substantiate my loyalty, let me confide to you that, on Christmas Day, I was approached by a Senator from a State of the same latitude as Mr. Thompson's, and wherein disunionist views are likewise proclaimed in public daily; this Senator, I swear, invited me to join a conspiracy, sir, to kidnap *you*, and to place Mr. Breckinridge in the Presidential chair! (*gasps and hubbub*) Mr. President, I indignantly refused, and from the same store of righteous indignation I hereby state that I cannot countenance your violation of solemn pledges respecting Fort Sumter!

BLACK: May we hope, Mr. Floyd, to construe this lack of countenance, with its imputations of grave disrespect, as the long-delayed fulfillment of our expectations that you resign the post you have administered with such notorious incompetence?

STANTON: You say incompetence; I say perfidy!

FLOYD: I am a sick man, or I would demand satisfaction.

STANTON: On that same Christmas Day when you were showing such loyalty to the President, this same President was obliged to countermand your order to ship cannon south from Pittsburgh—cannon, Mr. Floyd, ostensibly intended for a Texas fort in no way prepared to receive them! Thank God for the vigilance of my fellow-citizens of Pittsburgh!

BUCHANAN: Gentlemen, please, my head is spinning. In the

matter of the Charleston forts, we shall wait to hear from Major Anderson himself. He acted within the letter of his instructions, though against the trend of my policy. If in truth it appears he took alarm without cause, then we might consider restoring for the present the former status quo. *(He wearily sits down at his desk.)*

*All leave, dissatisfied.* BLACK *remains.*

BLACK: With some ingenuity, Mr. Buchanan, we have brought ourselves to stand upon a very narrow piece of ground.

BUCHANAN: It will suffice, if it serves to gain us time. Since Lincoln will not come to Washington, I have sent Duff Green to Springfield, to gain the assent of the President-elect to a new national constitutional convention. Green's first report strongly suggests that Lincoln is amenable. I pray that this be so. For a convention would become the voice of the people, who are overwhelmingly conservative, and whose letters pour in upon me like a hurricane of tears. Extend the Missouri Compromise line, and enforce the Fugitive Slave law—that is all we need for peace. By the hour I await Green to telegraph Lincoln's reprieving statement.

BLACK: But the Republican party was born of repugnance for the Missouri Compromise; the party is the freesoil delusion's very child. Lincoln can scarcely disavow his own platform. Fanaticism has secured in him its instrument.

BUCHANAN: But he will be *President.* If only he would come to Washington and smell the blood in the air! Seward now smells it, and was ready to assent to the Crittenden Compromise, until the radicals renewed their hold on Lincoln. Wall Street is panicked, and will exert restraint.

BLACK: But in no case will the Gulf States stay in.

BUCHANAN: True, the tide runs with the secessionists now. But when they find themselves isolated, when Virginia and Tennessee hold fast, that tide will turn. Time, Mr. Black, time. We must buy it by the month, and it is sold only by the hour.

BLACK: I fear the ground where you stand is so narrow, you cannot invite many to join you upon it.

BUCHANAN: The ground is narrow, as the top of a dike is narrow; it is narrow as the right path is always narrow!

BLACK: Mr. President, you are overwrought. I fear these pressures bear upon you cruelly.

BUCHANAN (*brushes at air*): They whittle me, it is true. But there is still some stick left. All things will pass. Once I was told I had a destiny, and now it is mine with a vengeance.

*Moment of darkness.*
*December 28th, 1860.*

BUCHANAN *and* BLACK *as before.* STANTON *enters, full of energy and insolence, announcing:* The South Carolina Commissioners, as they call themselves, are here. Were it mine to decide, Mr. President, I would refuse to entertain them.

BUCHANAN: They are honorable men, Mr. Stanton. I know them well, from happier days. (*stands to shake their hands*) Mr. Barnwell, Mr. Orr, Mr. Adams. I receive you as private gentlemen, and not as diplomatic agents. As I stated unmistakably in my message of December 3rd, Congress alone has the authority to decide what shall be the relations between the federal government and South Carolina.

ADAMS: We have the honor, Mr. President, to transmit to you a copy of the ordinance of secession by which the State of South Carolina has resumed the powers she once delegated to the government of the United States, and has now declared her perfect sovereignty and independence.

BUCHANAN: A well-worded document, I do not doubt. (*declines to accept it*)

ORR: Mr. President, in this very office, little more than a fortnight ago, you made a solemn pledge, as a gentleman, to maintain the status quo in Charleston harbor. Major Anderson has violated that pledge, and unless restitution is made a bloody issue is probable.

BUCHANAN: But, Mr. Orr, word has just arrived that the troops of Governor Pickens have now seized Castle Pinckney and Fort Moultrie. How can we order Major Anderson back, when the place to which he would return has been occupied by force? (*They cannot answer.*) I ask the question in a rhetorical sense merely, for it is not my office, nor my purpose, to negotiate with you.

BARNWELL: Mr. Buchanan, sir, we came here as the representatives of an authority which could at any time within the past sixty days have taken possession of the forts, but which, upon pledges given in a manner that we cannot doubt, determined to trust to your honor rather than to its own power. We urge upon you the immediate withdrawal of all the troops from the harbor of Charleston. They constitute a standing menace; their presence poisons negotiations that should be settled with temperance and judgment. Remove them, sir, to safeguard your own honor, and the welfare of the people who still accept your governance.

BUCHANAN: My honor is not at issue; I made no pledge; I distinctly recall stating that the President could not be bound by any proviso.

BARNWELL: An understanding was reached, sir, and Major Anderson, acting with or without your orders, has violated it.

Unless you act, the consequences will be dire. Withdrawal or war, sir. Choose.

BUCHANAN: Mr. Barnwell, you are pressing me too importunely. You don't give me time to consider. You don't give me time to say my prayers. I always say my prayers when required to act upon any great state affair. (*He seems senile, lost. The others are shocked.*)

BLACK (*hastily intervening*): The President wishes to terminate this interview. Gentlemen, we will give you your answer in writing.

*Blackout.*

*The Cabinet is meeting.* STANTON, BLACK, THOMPSON. *Floyd absent.* Toucey, Thomas, Holt *silent.* BUCHANAN *has removed his swallowtail Inauguration coat and sits slumped in a dressing gown.*

STANTON (*brandishing papers*): These gentlemen claim to be ambassadors. It is preposterous! They cannot be ambassadors; they are lawbreakers, traitors. They should be arrested. You cannot negotiate with them; and yet it seems by this paper that you have been led into doing that very thing. With all respect to you, Mr. President, I must say that the Attorney-General, under his oath of office, dares not be cognizant of the pending proceedings. Your reply to these so-called ambassadors must not be transmitted as the reply of the President. It is wholly unlawful and improper; its language is unguarded and to send it as an official document will bring the President to the verge of usurpation!

BUCHANAN (*feeble*): I will allow the urgency of the days, Mr. Stanton, to excuse the heat of your words. I hold out to the Commissioners the hope of submitting a proposal from them to the Congress. If they will retreat from Moultrie, and guarantee our federal property immunity for the rest of our administration, I see no harm in considering the restoration of Major Anderson to where he was five days ago.

THOMPSON: The subject for consideration, Mr. President, is the removal of Major Anderson from Charleston harbor entirely. I urge it upon you as the only sane and magnanimous course.

STANTON: For such magnanimity, they carve gallows-timber!

BLACK (*soothingly*): Mr. President, the language of this paper is self-incriminatory. It appears to concede the right of negotiation, when the ownership of federal forts is beyond negotiation. It implies that Major Anderson might be at fault in regard to a pledge made by you; when any such pledge or bargain should be flatly denied.

STANTON: Major Anderson is a hero, who saved this country when all else were paralyzed!

BLACK: Mr. Buchanan, you reiterate the Constitution's failure to specify a right of coercion, when what is meant is the right of our government to make war upon a State considered as a foreign country, *not* the right of the Chief Executive to defend federal property, or to put down those who resist federal officers performing their legal duties. You have always asserted your right of coercion to that extent. In your anxious, and laudable, desire to avoid civil war, you promote in these Carolina rebels dangerous illusions of power.

THOMPSON: Gentlemen, I resist the imputation that any rebellion has taken place. South Carolina's dissolution of its contract with the other States was carried forward with strict legality. (*They ignore him, as before.*)

BUCHANAN: Time, Mr. Black, let me gain time. Time is the great conservative force.

STANTON: Time does not preserve, it destroys. *Men* preserve!

BLACK: Time is not their enemy but ours. We speak of congressional prerogatives, but Congress has so many voices it owns none; the extremists cancel everything; this fall's Democratic victories have hardened the Republican minority to the point of wishing for secession. These Compromise plans are nothing but the natterings of moribund Whigs. Even the conservative press in the North rages against our failure to show force. General Scott urged reinforcements months ago; this administration committed a fatal error in not sending down troops enough to hold *all* the forts. But Sumter can still be saved. Two hundred fifty recruits can sail from New York tomorrow.

BUCHANAN (*distant, weak*): You speak of the forts as though they possessed real value. But their value now is chiefly symbolic.

STANTON: Precisely, sir. The South craves instruction from a confident show of firmness. Send troops to Sumter, send guns; and the Unionists even within the Palmetto State will rise up and scatter the secessionist illusion to the winds.

BUCHANAN: Such reinforcements . . . might be construed . . . I *did* affirm the status quo as my policy. (*rouses self*) It is essential, if war is to come, that we not appear to strike the first blow. Power does not flow from the government, in a nation constructed such as ours; it flows upward, from the people. If the people are to rally, it must be to a flag that has been wronged.

STANTON (*to* BLACK): A hand so timid of blood should never have touched the helm of State.

BUCHANAN (*continuing as in a dream*): I will not reinforce Anderson, nor will I withdraw him. I will not concede the right of secession, nor will I precipitate civil war.

STANTON (*to* BLACK): It is useless. We wrangle over a corpse.

*Blackout.*
*December 30th, 1860, a Sunday.*
*Church bells ring.* BUCHANAN *alone.* BLACK *enters.*

BLACK: You sent for me, Mr. President.

BUCHANAN: Yes, Mr. Black. Did you sleep well?

BLACK: Not at all, Mr. Buchanan. I spent a comfortless night.

BUCHANAN: And there is little news this morning to comfort us.

BLACK: What do you hear from Charleston?

BUCHANAN: Captain Humphreys has telegraphed that the arsenal too has been seized.

BLACK: And from Springfield?

BUCHANAN: Mr. Lincoln sends me silence.

BLACK *is silent.*

BUCHANAN: Is it true that you, too, talk of leaving me?

BLACK: It is true that I am going to resign.

BUCHANAN: I am overwhelmed to know that you of all other men are going to leave me in this crisis. You are from my own State, my closest political and personal friend. I have leaned upon you in these troubles as upon none other, and I insist that you shall stand by me to the end.

BLACK: Mr. President, from the start I had determined to stand by you to death and destruction if need be. There is no storm of popular indignation I would not breast by your side, no depth of misfortune into which I would not descend with you, provided you have a cause to defend. But your answer to the Commissioners leaves you no cause; it sweeps the ground from under our feet; it places you where no man can stand with you, and where you cannot stand alone. (*Bells continue; one is Buchanan's* BELL.)

BUCHANAN: You take this reply so much to heart? I thought to gain time for passions to subside, and for reason to resume her sway. We must not have an open rupture. We are not prepared for war, and if war is provoked, Congress cannot be relied upon to strengthen my arm, and the Union must utterly perish.

BLACK: That document is the powder that has blown your Cabinet to the four winds. It forces the Southern men out, and you cannot ask that we stay. I would not leave you for any earthly consideration so long as I could stay by you with self-respect, but I cannot do it, if the paper you have prepared is sent to the gentlemen from South Carolina.

BUCHANAN (*toys with paper, then flips it over*): I cannot part with you. Here, take this paper and modify it to suit yourself, but do it before the sun goes down. (*His* BELL *sounds.*)

*Blackout.*
*Cabinet meeting.*

THOMPSON: Mr. President, the South Carolina Commissioners have sent an answer to your response of December 30th.

BUCHANAN: Mr. Thompson, would you read it aloud.

*While* THOMPSON *stands en tableau, the voice of* ANNE COLEMAN, *amplified, reads from the wings:*

"My dear James Buchanan,

I have been informed, alas from a source I cannot doubt, that upon your recent return from away, ere that evening you deigned to visit me, you favored with a call Mrs. Jenkins and her sister Miss Grace Hubley, and lingered with them pleasantly abovewards of an hour. Such an incident, though not formidable in itself, confirms in painful manner the many intimations of negligence I have lately received from you. You plead preoccupation with the quantity of new legal business the national distress has laid upon you; and in truth the wife of a conscientious professional man must prepare to place herself, from time to time, accessory to his ambition. Yet the signs that so pain me arise in the realm of the spirit.

"Undoubtingly I scorned those voices close to me who insisted that the object of your regard was not my welfare but my riches. Your earnestness, your industry, your reticence, even your intervals of melancholy and self-distrust—such seemed to me the proper costume of a man's soul, a soul that might merge with mine, providing shelter to my frailty and substance to my imaginings. I opened to you as to none other, and as to none again—for each bud flowereth but once, though the tree flourish forever. With what dreadful fatality, then, with what terror and shame, have these autumnal weeks borne in upon me that my warmth accosts in you a deceptive coolness as unalterable as the mask of death. Had my affection been received by you as a treasure confided, and not as an adornment bestowed, you would not be flaunting your new prestige before the sisters Hubley nor flirting about Lancaster in the dozens of sprightly incidents obliging gossip reports to me. Did you love me, your bones of their gravity would have torn you from such unfaithful lightness.

"I foresee your protestations. I hear your voice, pleading circumstance. Believe me, the barrier to our happiness lies fixed beyond circumstance. Our engagement is broken. For myself, beyond this denial of him I loved dearest, I see an abyss only. I do not wish, nor, since you are a gentleman, do I expect, to meet you again.

In sorrow,<br>Anne"

THOMPSON *hands letter to* BUCHANAN.

BUCHANAN: How does the Cabinet vote that this message be received?

BLACK: It is insupportably insolent.

STANTON: Mr. President, it terms you a liar.

THOMPSON: Though the Commissioners have my sympathy, this answer is violent, unfounded, and disrespectful.

BUCHANAN: I will endorse it: "This paper, just presented to the President, is of such a character that he declines to receive it." (*puts down pen*) There. It is now over. (*softly, to* TOUCEY *and* HOLT, *so* THOMPSON *does not hear*) Reinforcements must be sent.

*Blackout. The next scene under stroboscopic light, like a bombardment. While* BUCHANAN *sits at his desk,* CABINET MEMBERS *rush in and out, acting as messengers:*

Georgia has seized Fort Pulaski!

Alabama has taken Fort Morgan!

The *Star of the West* has sailed from the Narrows!

Major Anderson sends word that reinforcement is not necessary!

Too late! The *Star of the West* cannot be called back!

THOMPSON: Mr. President, I have been deceived. I had no knowledge of any warship being sent to the Carolina coast. This is tantamount to war!

BUCHANAN: The orders were given, Mr. Thompson, within your hearing. I regret extremely that the troubles of the times have rendered it necessary for us to part; but whatever may be your future destiny, I shall ever feel a deep interest in your welfare and happiness.

HOLT: The *Star of the West* has been fired upon from the Charleston shore!

BUCHANAN: And not a gun on board! I knew we should have sent the *Brooklyn*, but that dropsical old dotard Scott talked me out of it! Tell me, did Major Anderson fire his batteries from Sumter in reply?

HOLT: No, he had no orders, and did not know that reinforcements were intended. The *Star of the West* has turned back!

BUCHANAN: Well, my lucky *Star*. It looks as though we might be handing Mr. Lincoln a full kettle after all! Send Anderson my official commendation.

*More messages:*

Mississippi has seceded!

Florida is gone!

BLACK: The Alabama convention, with Yancey at his most eloquent, voted for withdrawal, sixty-one to thirty-nine.

BUCHANAN: Thirty-nine Unionists in Alabama! There is still ground for compromise.

*Messages:*

Louisiana has passed its secession ordinance, 113 to 17!

And Texas is out, 166 to 8!

*Enter* CHARLES SUMNER, *the tall and handsome prince of Northern righteousness:* Mr. President, what can Massachusetts do for the good of the country?

BUCHANAN: Much, Mr. Sumner. No State more.

SUMNER: What is that?

BUCHANAN: Adopt the Crittenden proposition.

SUMNER: Is that necessary?

BUCHANAN: Yes.

SUMNER (*very erect*): Mr. President, Massachusetts has not yet spoken directly on these propositions. But I feel authorized to say—at least I give it as my opinion—that such are the unalterable convictions of the people, that they would see their State sunk below the sea and become a sandbank before they would adopt these propositions. (*Exit.*)

BLACK: The convention of the Confederate States of America, Howell Cobb presiding, has elected Jefferson Davis provisional President.

BUCHANAN: A good safe man. Toombs imbibes to excess, and Yancey inebriates himself with words. Poor Cobb, he must have thought the plum was his.

HARRIET *bustles in, carrying in her arms a large signed steel engraving, in heavy frame, of the young Queen Victoria. At first glance Victoria's head seems hers.*

HARRIET: Oh Nunc, get dressed, my goodness, everybody's so upset about the troops in Washington; some say you're setting up to be a military tyrant, and others say the Confederates are going to kidnap you and make Washington *their* capital instead of ours! Oh, and the clerks from the patent office spilled eggnog into the Chickering at their farewell party, and I *can't* find enough boxes for all the nice things Queen Victoria wanted us to have. Let me put this away from the window in case the shooting starts. (*sets it on the mantel*) Don't you think Mr. Lincoln looks like Robert Burns? He seems *so* well-spoken, but they say Mrs. L. is *aw*fully *western*—loud and unrefined. Oh, Nunc, it's been such *fun*—if Mr. Lincoln is shot, couldn't we stay?

BUCHANAN (*struggling out of his dressing gown and into his starlined coat*): "Il est plus difficile de s'empêcher d'être gouverné que de gouverner les autres."

HARRIET: I'm sorry, Nunc, the reflexive always confuses me, unless I see it on the page.

BUCHANAN: "Il est plus facile de paraître digne des emplois qu'on n'a pas que de ceux que l'on exerce."

HARRIET: Oh, Nunc, remember how we danced! (*dances off*)

BUCHANAN (*reciting at audience*): "Notre mérite nous attire l'estime des honnêtes gens, et notre étoile celle du public." (*puts on top hat, taps it*) I will ride to the Capitol with Old Abe whether I am assassinated or not.

BUCHANAN, *dressed for ceremony, stands facing audience. Strobe lights freeze for two bright seconds.*

*Blackout for five seconds.*

*Lights.* LINCOLN *stands in* BUCHANAN's *place; he is* GEORGE COLEMAN *with a beard. Three seconds.*

*Blackout.*

*Light gathers mistily at the podium, where* BUCHANAN *is giving a speech. March 6th, 1861.*

BUCHANAN: Mr. Mayor, my old neighbors, friends, and fellow citizens: I have not language to express the feelings which swell my heart on this occasion: but I do most cordially thank you for this demonstration of your personal kindness to an old man, who comes back to you ere long to go to his final rest. And here let me say that, having visited many foreign climes, my heart has ever turned to Lancaster as the spot where I would wish to live and die. When yet a young man, in far remote Russia, my heart was still with friends and neighbors in good old Lancaster. (*applause*)

I have come to lay my bones among you, and during the brief, intermediate period which Heaven may allot me, I shall endeavor to perform the duties of a good citizen, and a kind friend and neighbor. My advice shall be cheerfully extended to all who may seek it, and my sympathy and support shall never be withheld from the widow and the orphan. (*applause*)

I came to this city in 1809, more than half a century ago, and am, therefore, I may say, among your oldest citizens. When I parted from President Lincoln, on introducing him to the Executive Mansion, according to custom, I said to him, "If you are as happy, my dear sir, on entering this house as I am in leaving it and returning home, you are the happiest man in this country!" (*applause, and Curtain*)

# ACT III

*Wheatland again. The window dark as before. Washington's por-
trait is down, Anne's is back up, with the etching of Queen Victoria
still on the mantel, where* HARRIET *set it. The podium is again a
bed.* BUCHANAN *in bed, groaning. He is a dying man.*

BUCHANAN: . . . the horror . . .

HARRIET (*at foot of bed, a large scrapbook in her lap*): NUNC, it
   wasn't all bad. Shall I read to you from my scrapbook?

BUCHANAN: . . . the shame . . .

HARRIET (*cheerfully trying to deafen herself to his agony*): Here.
   The very first page. "The President-elect rode in an open
   carriage, surrounded by the Keystone Club, preceded by
   the military and a beautiful representation of the Goddess
   of Liberty upon a high platform drawn by six horses, and
   followed by a miniature ship-of-war of considerable size,
   which was made by the mechanics of the Washington Navy
   Yard. Beyond the fainting of a few ladies in the crowd, no
   incidents of an unpleasant nature occurred."

BUCHANAN *groans.*

HARRIET (*turning page*): Just two days later. "Another bright, clear day. The sunlight filtered through even into the cool, dim apartment of the Capitol basement which, beneath the throbbing discussions of Senate and House, was reserved for the Supreme Court. At eleven exactly, the procession of black-garbed judges moved from their robing room to the chamber, the younger members, as they kicked up the long gowns with their heels, adjusting their gait to that of the tremulous chief, Roger B. Taney. The Chief Justice, gathering his papers before him, began reading in a high, thin voice the Supreme Tribunal's decision in the case of one Dred Scott, a slave—"

BUCHANAN: The horror!

HARRIET: Here's something amusing, Nunc. On the night of July 14th, 1857, the "Dead Rabbits" and the "Bowery Boys," competing gangs of hoodlums, staged a memorable battle at Bayard and Elizabeth Streets, New York City. The following night, fighting broke out at Five Points near the Mission House. (*turns page*) On July 10th of the following year, in Lexington, Kentucky, "one William Barker stabbed the city marshal and was jailed. A crowd gathered and seized the prisoner; a beam was pushed out from a second-story window of the court house, and Barker was soon swinging from the end of a rope."

BUCHANAN *grimaces and writhes.*

HARRIET: In March of 1859, the river steamer *Princess*, on the Mississippi near Baton Rouge, exploded, killing two hundred persons and blacks. In May, a tornado passed through Iowa, leaving a trail of ruin in its wake; even the seedling corn stalks were torn from the ground. That same month, a shaft of the Blue Rock Coal Mine, near Zanesville, Ohio,

caved in, burying a number of miners. On June 27th—
Nunc, were you aware of all this?—a train wreck on the
Michigan Southern Railroad near South Bend, Indiana,
took some forty lives.

BUCHANAN (*not to her*): God!

HARRIET (*turning pages*): This will cheer you up. "Late in 1857,
a party of topographical engineers under Lieutenant Joseph C. Ives commenced exploration of the Colorado
River. On April 5th, 1858, Ives came upon the Grand Can-
yon in all its hitherto-unimagined sublimity."

BUCHANAN: The abyss.

HARRIET: This is even nicer, Nunc. "Under President Pierce,
Congress appropriated thirty thousand dollars for the purchase of thirty-five camels in Egypt. In 1857, during the
Presidency of James Buchanan, the first American camel
train left Fort Defiance, New Mexico, and successfully arrived in California. Though the camels managed excel-
lently, the American drivers found them resistant to
direction and disagreeable, and the unobliging beasts spent
the remainder of their days running wild, or hauling salt in
Death Valley."

BUCHANAN *twists in pain.*

HARRIET: Here's one you'll remember. "On August 5th, 1858,
the British ship *Agamemnon* and the United States frigate
*Niagara*, by the method of meeting in mid-Atlantic, splic-
ing, and sailing in opposite directions, succeeded in laying
a telegraph cable from Ireland to Newfoundland. President
Buchanan received a congratulatory message from Queen
Victoria but, fearing a hoax, delayed his reply. When his
reply had been prepared, the underseas cable had unac-
countably fallen silent, and all attempts to revive transmis-
sion failed."

BUCHANAN: The abyss.

HARRIET: Here's another cable story. "On June 30th, 1859, the French tightrope *artiste* Charles Blondin thrilled and edified an immense throng of spectators by crossing a thousand-foot cable strung high above Niagara Falls. At about the same time, the first Pullman cars were put into service."

BUCHANAN (*not to her*): Why, Lord? Why?

HARRIET: "In the winter of 1858–59, stories began to circulate concerning fabulous gold discoveries in the region of Kansas around Pike's Peak."

BUCHANAN *groans*.

HARRIET (*flipping pages*): Nunc, do you want to hear about Colonel Wright's massacre of the Yakima Indians? Or the Mountain Meadows massacre committed by the Mormons? Or John Brown's raid at Harper's Ferry?

BUCHANAN (*looking at her at last*): John—Brown.

HARRIET: This will please you, Nunc. "On December 2nd, 1859, the venerable horsethief, murderer, traitor, and Negro-lover John Brown thrilled and edified an immense throng of spectators at Charleston, Virginia, by being hung by the neck until dead. Brown won the respect of all in attendance as he comported himself with great dignity to the last."

BUCHANAN: Ah! (*closes eyes, is calmer when he opens them*) Old Brown turned a good profit out of his dying. If Wise had been wise, he would have let him live, as a crazy man. Does it say there—the day of his death, he wrote some words.

LINCOLN *enters and recites:* I John Brown am now quite certain that the crimes of this guilty land will never be purged away but with blood. I had as I now think vainly flattered myself that without very much bloodshed it might be done.

BUCHANAN (*still in pain*): Aye, and so it proved, and the last blood was yours. Mr. Lincoln, if you were as happy entering eternity as I shall be in leaving this life, you were a happy man indeed.

LINCOLN (*courteously*): Mr. President, I cannot say that I shall enter it with much pleasure, but I assure you that I shall do what I can to maintain the high standards set by my illustrious predecessors who have occupied it.

BUCHANAN: Slidell was right, of course. He was never wrong, Slidell. I delivered the South to you like a lamb pegged by one foot. Sumter was the peg. The trick was, to make the lamb appear a wolf. Once the North could call itself righteous, then human greed could have its space, and the rest was but a long and bloody grinding down. You and Douglas were wrong to chaff me over Lecompton; Lecompton was the key. By yielding, I led her deeper in. Her assets—her generals, her sharp-shooters, *sa belle folie*—were as ready in '57 as in '61; the North in '57 was staggered by the panic. For every day my administration staved off secession, another factory sprouted. I loved the South, Mr. Lincoln, and she loved me, but I gulled her. By the time she unsheathed her dress sword, the other side had a bludgeon. And they say Butcher Grant is to be the next President.

LINCOLN *says nothing.* BUCHANAN *grows alarmed.*

BUCHANAN: Miss Hetty! Miss Hetty!

MISS HETTY *enters.*

BUCHANAN (*confidentially*): Without appearing discourteous, ask this tall petitioner to go away. He smells of blood.

MISS HETTY: There is no one here, Mr. Buchanan. (*It is true.*) Just you and me and Miss Harriet, as it's always been.

BUCHANAN: Tell me, Miss Hetty—tell me frankly, without fear of giving offense—does that bank in Pottsville still issue bogus notes featuring my face, with a rope about my neck, and the word *Judas* inscribed across my forehead?

MISS HETTY: Ah, no, Mr. Buchanan, that was the bitterness during the war. It's years since, nobody mentions you now, the talk in Lancaster is all Mr. Stevens and how the failure to convict the President is killing him sure as God's hand.

BUCHANAN: And are the Masons still standing guard duty about the house, lest a lynch mob arrive?

MISS HETTY: You're living in the old times, Mr. Buchanan. Now the mobs that come to the door are visiting glee clubs, and the Lancaster firemen when word gets about you've laid in a fresh stock of whiskey.

BUCHANAN (*sitting up*): And do they still whisper, in Lancaster, that I killed Anne Coleman?

MISS HETTY (*primly*): That was before my time, Mr. Buchanan. I never made the good lady's acquaintance.

BUCHANAN (*straining closer*): And is it true, as messengers assure me, that Miss Harriet has fallen prey to fornication?

HARRIET: What did you say about me, Nunc? Can't you sleep? You seem so restless.

BUCHANAN: I have all my accounts to check. Judge Black has bought the old farm in Mercersburg, but he gave me ten cents too little. Dr. Yates and Maria continue extravagant. And the New York bankers do not trust Thomas because he's from Maryland; he offered twelve per cent on five million, and only half was bid for.

HARRIET: Have you heard your Jay's Exercise for the day?

BUCHANAN: Do you forgive me, for placing you to school with the nuns at Georgetown? I would not have done it, but that I gauged your Protestant principles were settled beyond the possibility of corruption.

HARRIET (*reads*): "May thirty-first. That by two immutable

things, in which it was impossible for God to lie, we might have a strong consolation, who have fled for refuge to lay hold upon the hope set before us. Hebrews six, eighteen."

BUCHANAN: Two immutable things? "La fortune et l'humeur gouvernent le monde." "La soleil ni la mort ne se peuvent regarder fixement."

HARRIET: Do you want the Commentary, Nunc?

BUCHANAN: Only if it will not dismay me.

HARRIET: "One of these two things was his promise, the other was his oath. The Apostle acknowledges that *both* of them were immutable. Why then was the latter added to the former?"

BUCHANAN: Why indeed? Trust Jay to spin a straight web.

HARRIET: "Not to *constitute*, but to *show* the immutability of his counsel."

BUCHANAN: Did you hear a bell? I expect Swarr every moment.

HARRIET: " 'As I live, saith the Lord, I have no pleasure in the death of him that dieth.' "

BUCHANAN: A hard saying. One of the many hard sayings in that dark book. I will make a confession to you. I dislike the Bible. I have disliked it ever since the childish days when I would watch my mother strain her dear pure eyes to make out the meaning in the tangled columns of that mighty tribal anthology. By the cruel light of flaming splinters thrust between the fieldstones of the fireplace, she would read this same volume here by my bedside. Ignoring my silent longing for her voice, she would dote upon that book as upon a black mirror. Ever since her death, I have carried it with me, though its weight is leaden. Israel's ark, America's millstone. Give me, instead, light, clear things: arithmetic and legal logic, whiskey and springwater, Russian amber and British manners, the French language and Japanese porcelain. Give me translucence and air, Tit, and a tingle on the tongue!

HARRIET: Nunc, am I tiring you?

BUCHANAN: "On s'ennuie presque toujours avec deux que l'on ennuie."

HARRIET: I must say, Nunc, I find these exercises exceedingly dry and Presbyterian. This man would niggle us into Paradise.

BUCHANAN: He has his claws, however. You may stop when he shows them.

HARRIET (*reading*): "We first see how hard it is to comfort the conscience, and to inspire us with 'a strong consolation,' not only while we are fleeing for refuge to lay hold on the hope set before us, but even after we *have* fled. We have a controversy with God, and we know that he has much ground against us; and a consciousness of guilt makes us timid and suspicious."

BUCHANAN: Stop, my love. There you may stop. We have a controversy with God, verily. I know, for all of my life He has been sending me letters of reprimand.

*Enter* JAMES BUCHANAN, *his father, played by the same actor who played* DOUGLAS *and* ROBERT COLEMAN. *Dark clothes. A wrathful heaviness.*

FATHER: James.

BUCHANAN: Yes, Father? How can I please you?

FATHER: There is but one path to pleasing me, and that is the path of obedience to God. Shortly ago this communication was delivered to our door. Kindly read it.

BUCHANAN: It is Dr. Davidson's hand. (*As he reads, shock drains his face.*) This cannot be.

FATHER: Aye; nor can the dead die. (*turns back and remains motionless*)

BUCHANAN (*falling back into pillows*): The shame!

ELIZABETH BUCHANAN (*entering*): Jamie, whatever under Heaven! Your father is telling me Dickinson College wishes to see no more of ye; yet you've been proclaiming yourself to me as the foremost scholar of the class.

BUCHANAN: Mother, I swear to you, this is as unexpected as it is undeserved.

MOTHER (*reading*): ". . . disorderly conduct . . . repeated manifestations of disrespect . . . pursuits of dissipation and lewdness in the public places of Carlisle. But for the high respect the faculty and trustees entertain for the name of James Buchanan . . . We decline, however, to receive him as a student for the term coming . . ."

BUCHANAN: Dr. Davidson should have reproached me on those occasions when my conduct warranted. The college is profuse with extravagance and mischief; in its deteriorated condition it enforces discipline so feebly that my instinctive deportment, which was dutiful and sober, became conspicuous cause for ridicule. If I allowed myself to transgress against propriety, it was not from any natural tendency toward immoderation, but to conform with the life around me. I was never deficient in my studies, as my August examinations bear witness. This letter (*begins crying*) mortifies me.

MOTHER (*hugging him*): Ah now Jamie, this is but a little thing, compared to what could be. A lark or two go into the making of a man.

BUCHANAN: Father (*sobs*), Father could not speak, he was so angry. He will never speak to me again.

MOTHER: Ah now yes he will, anger is like cider, it kenna keep. How could a man stay angry at his eldest son, that is so much of himself? Disappointed it may be, but your father's too steady ever to be ruled by wrath.

BUCHANAN: He *never* praises me! No matter how worthily I perform, he sets me the next task without a word of gratification.

MOTHER: No more does he praise himself, Jamie. It's not his way. He loves ye with a terrible heart, take it on faith from your mother.

BUCHANAN: Let him speak to me direct. I'm *glad* of this disgrace; now that Dickinson is done with me, I can stay home all day, steal whiskey and snuff from the store, and be a Mercersburg lout with the others. No; better yet, I'll go west, and trade in guns and furs, and be tortured to death by the Cherokees. *Then* he'll miss the boy I was.

MOTHER: Ah, don't take on so blasphemously. No matter what befalls ye, never be hopeless, and never be ungrateful. How does the primer say?—Job feels the Rod, Yet blesses God. Your father is everything that is to the both of us.

BUCHANAN: I don't hate my father; but I *do* hate his silence.

MOTHER: No, now, and ye can't; his silence is his strength, and his strength is his sweetness. In this letter, both father and son have been badly used, 'tis mine opinion, by a schoolmaster outsmarted more often than was prudent, Jamie. Write Reverend King. He's known us in sorrow and joy, and now he heads up the Trustees of Dickinson College. Confess your remorse. Pledge yourself to better behavior, and I don't doubt but he'll manage your readmission. It's a struggling little school these days, and the Buchanans are paying customers.

BUCHANAN: I feel no remorse. I did nothing others were not guilty of, but their mediocrity shielded them. The faculty is jealous of its own prestige. Because I am foremost and a leader, I am singled out for rebuke. It is petty. It is unjust.

MOTHER (*seductive*): Come, Jamie, don't be counting all the rights and wrongs of it. Lucifer in his beauty had a grievance as well. Penitence is the Christian way; Jesus brought the news, we're none of us all in the right.

BUCHANAN: Father is never penitent.

MOTHER: He is a rougher man than you are shaping to be; for the sake of your parents' love, don't throw your life away. Go to Reverend King.

BUCHANAN: For the sake of peace, I will. But—

MOTHER: But what, my little Jamie boy?

BUCHANAN (*crying again*): I cannot forgive this.

*His mother stands back;* SUSANNA KEITT *enters, in a torn white dress, weeping. She flings herself on his bed.*

BUCHANAN: What have they done to you, child?

SUSANNA: They killed Mr. Keitt! My husband is *dead!* Leading a charge on the Yankees at Cold Harbor, his great heart took a wound and bled itself away. It was today, June the first. His beautiful body went back to dust. In ways that shame forbids me to describe, he was a god.

JAMES BUCHANAN, SR., *turns around and steps toward them.*

FATHER: Is this the same fire-eater Keitt who held back those who would have intervened when Bully Brooks beat Sumner senseless with a cane?

SUSANNA: He was a passionate man, but generous and gentle to me.

FATHER: Easy enough, to smile on those that cater to our lust. For the sake of his pride and ambition, thousands of less presuming men have perished. I have no pleasure in the death of him that dieth.

SUSANNA: Mr. Buchanan, who is this officer?

BUCHANAN: I do not know. He is a stranger to me.

SUSANNA: Mr. President, order him to leave us.

BUCHANAN: Dear child, I cannot. Naught in the Constitution explicitly sanctions such an order.

SUSANNA: For my sake, please. I am frightened. I am alone.

BUCHANAN (*feebly*): Turn back.

FATHER: I have taken a through ticket, and checked all my baggage. (*comes a step closer*)

SUSANNA: Protect me, Mr. Buchanan. He wishes to make me his.

FATHER (*with false friendliness, from which both cringe*): My daughter tells me I am acting too much the dragon.

SUSANNA (*to BUCHANAN*): I think he is the beast.

BUCHANAN: Hush. He is our father, child. (*strokes her head comfortingly*)

SUSANNA (*leaning her head against his chest*): You are my heart's light.

BUCHANAN: There is a darkness I have always feared. You bring me to its verge. I am grateful.

SUSANNA: Touch me.

BUCHANAN: Have I the right?

SUSANNA: It is true, what men say. You are cold.

BUCHANAN: Nay, warm. Danger flows from me like lava.

SUSANNA: Touch me, but lightly.

BUCHANAN (*continuing to stroke her hair*): Are you so alone?

SUSANNA: I have two daughters. No, I have one. Little Stella died the year the war was over. Mr. Keitt was a man, and no man is innocent, but my baby, stiff in my arms; I picked her up, and she was all one piece. Why, Mr. Buchanan? Who is to blame?

BUCHANAN (*so as not to be heard by the other*): I know, but am not at liberty to say.

SUSANNA (*pointing at* FATHER): That one! Him!

BUCHANAN (*pulls her arm down, frightened*): Do nothing to attract his attention.

SUSANNA: Only whisper to me, is he not our murderer and the lord of all betrayers?

BUCHANAN (*in pain*): To bring formal indictment—would exceed my vested authority. But let me satisfy you at least of this: I have been falsely accused.

SUSANNA: Oh, Mr. President, I always knew you were kind. I remember Mr. Cobb used to say, you were the best friend the South ever had!

BUCHANAN: You admit to another daughter?

SUSANNA: Oh, yes. Here is the honey darling.

ANN COOK *enters, bringing him water.*

BUCHANAN: Thank you, my child. Was it dark and cold, down by the spring?

GIRL: Yes, sah.

BUCHANAN: And do you still love me, as formerly?

GIRL: Yes, sah.

BUCHANAN: Or has time eroded your love, as it does all matter, simple and compound? Time does not halt, as once I thought, at the lip of the grave. The mound of earth settles, the wind scatters seed.

GIRL: Yes, sah.

BUCHANAN: I never thought, you must understand, slavery anything but an evil; I merely maintained that the Constitution in its wisdom provided for its protection.

SUSANNA (*hugging* ANN): Isn't she radiant? Isn't she glorious?

BUCHANAN: She is all we have prayed for. I promise you, the paternal role is one to which both inclination and experience fit me. I was the eldest child, once dear Mary was gathered in, of an ever-fecund mother. Jane and Maria, Sarah and Elizabeth, all were lulled by my rocking, whilst our mother napped. You shall not find me sluggard, when the midnight summons comes. (*His* BELL *rings.*)

GIRL: My mudder, de man beat her wid a coal shovel and cracked the side of her head (*shows*) here.

FATHER (*stepping forward*): Had you ever been a married man, Mr. President, you might know that a firm rebuke is a greater kindness to a wife, and more encourages her love, than a supine indulgence.

BUCHANAN: Satan! A universe engendered on such principles cries for a new caucus.

FATHER: Death and fornication, Jamie, are the most natural things in the world.

BUCHANAN: I perceive little natural about either one. Both are excrescences, grafted upon Nature by some agency perverted and alien.

FATHER (*laughs*): All Washington whispers, you have no need to shave. Your withered old cheek is as hairless as a girl's. Doughface indeed! (*laughs*)

BUCHANAN (*bowing head*): Father, forgive me.

GIRL: De water is fresh and good. A big frog jumped in de dark when I was fetching, but I tol myself, Don't you be scared, dere ain't no such things.

BUCHANAN (*looks at her in surprise*): Of course! A person can't be property. I must write Grier and tell him. Alas, it's too late, isn't it? Taney is dead. The court has delivered its judgment.

SUSANNA: Oh, Jim, Jim, I get so fearful. Tell him to go away. Promise me there is no death.

BUCHANAN: I can make no binding pledge, merely treat with the gentleman as a gentleman. (*to her, urgently, conspiratori-*

*ally*) Stay by my side, you tender ball of lechery, and I will quibble us both into Paradise.

*Enter* REVEREND WILLIAM PAXTON, *played by the actor who was* BLACK *and* EDWARD BUCHANAN. *Throughout their discourse,* SU-SANNA *sleeps by Buchanan's side.* ANN COOK *and* FATHER *withdraw but remain onstage.*

*The time is August, 1860.*

PAXTON: You sent for me, Mr. President.

BUCHANAN: I sent for you, Reverend Paxton, to request that you will favor me with a conversation upon the subject of religion. I knew your father and mother in early life, and, as you have some knowledge of my family, you are aware that I was religiously educated. But for some years I have been much more thoughtful than formerly upon religious subjects. I have never had any one with whom I have felt disposed to converse, but now that I find you here, at Bedford Springs, I have thought that you would understand my feelings, and that I would venture to open my mind to you upon this important subject, and ask for an explanation of some things that I do not clearly understand.

PAXTON: Mr. Buchanan, as you doubtless know, I do not agree with you in politics, nor feel great sympathy for your public career. Yet I have never entertained a doubt of your honesty, and it would gratify me, as a pastor and as your private acquaintance, to have such a conversation.

BUCHANAN: Will you, then, be good enough to explain to me what an experience of religion is?

PAXTON: My good sir!—the question disconcerts me with its breadth. Religious experience, at its most ecstatic and convulsive, finds description in the Gospels, as witness the conversion of St. Paul, the apparition of the risen Christ to the several Apostles, and the miraculous phenomena recorded in the Book of Acts. Homelier counterparts of these manifestations, most notoriously glossolalia, are encountered among enthusiastic American Christians, and the Roman hierarchy, of course, inflicts upon Latin peasantry a carnival of superstitious delusions—some of which, it is true, baffle rational explanation. But, all wonders aside, in the normal tenderness of father to child, of man to wife, of poet, if you will, toward natural splendor, we experience intimations of divinity—indeed, all our experience warrants the epithet "religious," insofar as the very existence of human mind and emotion gives the lie to any merely mechanistic explication of the universe. The ingenious Newton himself aspired above all to serve as an evangelist of the Lord.

BUCHANAN: Your points, Reverend Paxton, are all persuasive, though none is new to me, and none, I fear, banish all doubt. That there appears to be something immaterial about our circumstances, may be the product of our insufficient understanding of matter. What of these curious electrical properties, that so engage the physicists of England? And but lately, I believe, an abyss has appeared within the biological doctrine of the fixity of the species. In order to frame to you the sensation I would seek, let me confess the sensations I do have. Though I converse, rejoice, and weep among my fellow men, and although through accurate perception of their limitations and of my own possibilities I have achieved supreme office among them, yet as well as the executor of my life I am its witness, who witnesses unmoved. This inner witness is enclosed within my destiny as within a crystal container of a certain shape—a shape (*He demonstrates with pantomime.*) I discover by contact and abrasion, but which I am powerless to alter. I do not mean, good sir, that I am incapable of action in the common sense; in public as in private life, I have developed policies—policies which, I solemnly assure you, are those best favored to preserve the Union and, if it inevitably rupture, will aid time to mend it. No; but in a sphere above flat decision and consequence, in the sphere shall we say of *quintessence*, I am unable to join my inner self to this outer, public, Presidential self, who acts. This actor seems Another, who belongs to a realm coarsely removed from that wherein my true self dwells. Between my self and my deeds I feel always the gap of imposture. Now, do all men share this sensation, or is it peculiar to this one lost soul? For such a sense of impotent detachment and cool fatality—is it not despair, the very opposite of grace, and proof certain of damnation? I am earnest in this.

PAXTON: Your earnestness, sir, is evident, and should *per se* temper your cruel fears of damnation. "The bruised reed he will not break: the smoking flax he will not quench." I am somewhat astonished, indeed, at how little you have permitted the customary consolations of religion to permeate your reflectiveness. You would constitute your philosophy upon the most elemental premises. Were you denied, in childhood, instruction and example in Christian practice?

BUCHANAN: My mother's piety was as little flawed as my father's righteousness. Their twin example, it may be, served to alert me to my own recalcitrant imperfection. My adult life has brought me into association with many men—of whom General Jackson was the greatest—devoid, to all appearances, of inward division; their hearts and deeds were one. Always, in the presence of such men, I have marvelled, as a frog might marvel in the presence of eagles. And history marvels also; posterity bestrews their graves with flowers, though their palpable legacy is tyranny, confusion, and pain.

PAXTON: Mr. Buchanan, beneath the humility of your self-description, my ear, sharpened by many confessions, detects an overweening grievance. Do you question that the world as the Lord created it is good?

BUCHANAN *is wordless.*

PAXTON (*kindly*): Let me circumvent your silence by asking, rather, Do you doubt the Biblical account whereby our estate is a fallen estate, sunk in sin inextricably, and all our human efforts at improvement but a worming deeper into the mire?

BUCHANAN: No. The world is plainly such.

PAXTON: Do you then question the need for regeneration through the spirit that eternally abides, and the need of atonement through the sacrifice of our Lord Jesus Christ?

BUCHANAN: Did I doubt such need, I could rest complacent, like many a European atheist, in my failure to hold within me any certainty of redeeming faith.

PAXTON: Yet those men, such as the immortal Jackson, who were certainty embodied, you denigrate by the terms of your praise; for seen through the eyes of a frog an eagle must appear ridiculous, and its flight and ferocity superfluous. You profess awe before them; in truth you disdain these heroes as brutes of delusion and spendthrifts of blood. You disdain, indeed, the vital world, and therewith Creation's living God!

BUCHANAN: My tongue is disposed to protest; for I have ever been diligent in my prayers, and scrupulous in my duties.

But let my soul stand mute at the indictment. What then am I to do? How shall I become a Christian? I have summoned you in my lost condition for guidance, and you confirm me in apostasy.

PAXTON: You confirm yourself, Mr. Buchanan, and you can convert yourself to true belief with a single motion of the spirit. It is a matter of willing, not of opinion. God lives; we do not doubt, we accuse. In the guise of unbelief you bear an active grudge. Remove that grudge. Break this man of crystal who encloses you. Repent. Submit. Rejoice.

BUCHANAN: Do I dare rejoice, when men beg madness to rule them, and death reaps the only lasting harvest? When the nation, its tiller broken in my hand, veers toward cataclysm?

PAXTON: I will leave it to the editorialists of the New York *Tribune* to rebuke the pro-slavery equivocation which has brought us to these present ominous days. In my pastoral office let me urge upon you that the madness men follow is but the distorted image of something glorious.

BUCHANAN: I am not troubled by the sins of men, who are feeble; I am troubled by the sins of God, who is mighty.

FATHER (*shaking fist*): If we could hang that blaspheming old fool from the White House flagpole, the nation would have a holiday to outracket the Fourth! Die, Buchanan, and give us excuse for a clambake!

PAXTON: "Hast thou with him spread out the sky, which is strong, and as a molten looking glass?" Creation brooks not our questioning. It proceeds by eruption and revolution; otherwise all will stand rotten on undisturbed roots. Does no benefit emerge from volcanoes and plagues? "Touching the Almighty, we cannot find him out: he is excellent in power, and in judgment."

BUCHANAN: This levels too much. You would make all events benevolent.

PAXTON: And you would make them all malign. And so, by Adam's fall, they are. But what of Christ's sacrifice? You wish for sensations: well, in the darkness of prayer have you never felt God like a listening father bend close? Has your outward piety never proved an inward comfort? Has not the Lord in truth proved himself a constant partner and King of Love?

BUCHANAN: Could you give me again the text you first quoted—"The bruised reed—"

PAXTON: "The bruised reed he will not break; the smoking flax he will not quench, till he send forth judgment unto victory. And in his name shall the Gentiles trust." Matthew, quoting Isaiah. A pledge of charity extending from the Old Testament to the New. You are no stranger to holy emotions, Mr. Buchanan—the renewal of strength that devotions bestow, the serenity that follows upon repentance, the jubilance with which faith enriches the mundane. In the eyes of your personal acquaintance you have long been the model of a Christian; imitate their trust, and confirm yourself one.

BUCHANAN: My lack of experimental sensation of salvation would not be an impediment to my admission to Christian fellowship?

PAXTON: Your *professed* lack, Mr. President; were you less strict in conscience, you would have detected within yourself signs of grace a thousand times over.

BUCHANAN: My understanding was, the signs were unambiguous.

PAXTON: There is no sign, sir, the Devil cannot taint, if a flaw in our faith permit him to enter.

BUCHANAN (*having pondered*): Well, sir, I thank you. My mind is now made up. I hope that I am a Christian. I think I have much of the experience which you describe, and, as soon as I retire from my office as President, I will unite with the Presbyterian Church.

PAXTON: Why not now, Mr. President? God's invitation is *now*, and you should not say tomorrow.

BUCHANAN (*strong gesture*): I must delay, for the honor of religion. If I were to unite with the Church now, they would say "Hypocrite" from Maine to Georgia.

SUSANNA *stirs*. PAXTON *departs*.

SUSANNA (*sleepily*): Have you secured our eternal union?

BUCHANAN: No, I have been talking idly, with a very worldly man.

FATHER: Hypocrite!

BUCHANAN: "Il est plus aisé de connaître l'homme en général, que de connaître un homme en particulier."

FATHER: Seduce this child no longer, you pustulant bag of aphorisms and gout, you everlasting sluice of feeble piety and slippery dodges!

BUCHANAN: I loved her. I love her.

FATHER: Indeed and dandy, and many another, and every daughter of them come to a sorry end. What of Rose O'Neal Greenhow, the belle of slavocratic Washington, drowned in service as a Confederate spy?—sunk like a stone off Fort Fisher, her pockets weighted with the gold sovereigns earned by her prison memoirs!

*Enter* SLAYMAKER *and* REYNOLDS.

SLAYMAKER: And what of sweet Liz Craig, the prettiest widow in Athens, Georgia, come in mourning to Washington to snare the President? The old rake boarded her at the White House until she wearied of wooing the embodiment of shiftiness and married a man from Chicago, where the cold off Lake Michigan and the taunts of her Dixie-hating step-children bade her gentle heart cease this January last.

BUCHANAN (*groans*): Ah, dear Elizabeth. I lay awake dreaming my way to her room, when I should have been pondering Kansas.

FATHER: And what of Grace Hubley, so beguiled by an afternoon's tea she led a life of foolish flirtation thereafter, and perished whimpering like one of the damned when her careless gown caught fire from a coal grate!

REYNOLDS: And what of Mary Kittera Snyder, ignorant child primed to become the bride of a Senator, then scorned in the end, as were they all, though the old bull prated of marriage like a Valentine!

BUCHANAN: My family objected, they did not wish to share my estate—

SLAYMAKER: And after that, little Anna Payne, the niece of Dolley Madison, dismissed with a spattering of doggerel.

BUCHANAN *sits up in bed to recite:*

"In thee my chilled and blighted heart has found
A green spot in the dreary waste around.
Oh! that my fate in youthful days had been
T'have lived with such a one, unknown, unseen,
Loving and lov'd, t'have passed away our days
Sequestered from the world's malignant gaze!"

*All laugh, except* SUSANNA.

REYNOLDS: And what of Queen Victoria, a helpless widow since '61, and this retired functionary too mean-spirited to offer his suit and sire a transatlantic dynasty!

SLAYMAKER: Not to mention the Empress of Russia, whose heart he whirled to dizziness as a young buck fresh from Penn's forest, then left her encircled by assassins, her snow palace turning to tears with the warmth of her sighs!

MOTHER (*coming forward*): Ah, Jamie, can't you say No to President Jackson? For if ye take your eyes and ears to the court of Petersburg, do not expect to see me in the flesh again. Give your ambition a rest; your career already should gratify your pride. Your father's dead, and your favorite brother's poorly; dinna disappoint me. Stay. Your mother begs ye, Jamie.

FATHER: Madame, waste no more tears importuning this villain. His soul has been hardened by a sin beyond forgiveness. He got my wee daughter with child, and drove her to drink opium rather than face abandonment and shame.

MOTHER: Ah no, I will not hear it! (*runs from stage*)

BUCHANAN ( *feebly, in pain*): No . . . the most vicious . . . of rumors . . . Anne was a virgin . . . is still . . . we are both . . . virgins.

*Enter* SAMUEL W. BLACK, *an incongruous, overexcited figure in the dress of the 1850s, unaccustomed to public oratory, but gathering confidence as he goes, addressing first the deathbed visitants, and then, from the stage edge, the audience.*

SAMUEL BLACK: Excuse me, the name is Black, not Judge Black, a lesser shade as it were, a lesser shade of black—some might name me Gray. I am appointed by the unanimous request of my State delegation to return thanks from the very heart of Pennsylvania for this unprecedented vote for her own beloved son. (*polite applause*) I will not make a set speech. (SLAYMAKER *cheers,* "*Hooray!*") But we do return you all our humble, but our earnest, sincere gratitude, for the honor this day received at your hands. (*more applause*) Gentlemen, I said that I would not weary you with a set speech, and your kindling enthusiasm shall not make me forgetful; but one thing more and I will conclude. (*applause*) I have become identified with the female movement on this floor (*laughter*) from my support of the right of the ladies to the galleries. Now let me set Mr. Buchanan right on the matrimonial question.

SLAYMAKER: Hurrah! Hurrah for old Buck!

SAMUEL BLACK: Though our beloved chieftain has not, in his own person, exactly (*laughter*) fulfilled in his own person (*more laughter*) the duties that every man owes to the sex and to society, there is a reason. (*dramatic pause*) Ever since James Buchanan was a marrying man, he has been wedded to the CONSTITUTION, *and in Pennsylvania we do not allow bigamy!*

*Here, where Murat Halstead, reporting this moment of the Cincinnati Convention, wrote, "The convention flings its hats to the ceiling," the director of this play must arrange a demonstration to suit himself. Those on stage might be joined by others bearing placards, and all march about the bed. Ideally, the theatre audience would be caught up in the enthusiasm. When it subsides,* HARRIET, SUSANNA/ ANNE, *and the* FATHER *are left on stage with the dying man.*

BUCHANAN: Ach, the muddle . . . the horror . . .

FATHER *beckons. Obediently* ANNE *rises from* BUCHANAN'S *bed. He is slow to react, and gropes where she has been.*

BUCHANAN: Where have you gone?

ANNE (*at foot of bed*): I must leave you.

BUCHANAN (*pointing at* FATHER): Not with *him.*

ANNE: He wants me. He is not afraid of me.

BUCHANAN: But he is death.

ANNE: But he *does* things. He makes things happen. He fills me. Jim: goodbye.

BUCHANAN: Oh, stay! (*reaches out*)

ANNE *exits on the arm of the other.*

HARRIET: Nunc, would you mind awfully if I went too? It's been wonderful, being back at Wheatland again—remember all the hayrides? remember the squirrel we tried to save?—but Mr. Johnston needs me in just so many little ways, I can't begin to tell you. Here's a kiss and a hug, for the nicest old uncle a girl ever had.

BUCHANAN (*hoarsely, oppressed by her embrace*): Doucement, doucement. You feel heavy as earth upon me.

HARRIET (*standing erect, offended*): Silly!

*When she is gone,* BUCHANAN *groans, and groans again.* MISS HETTY *rushes in, smoothing her apron, tucking back her hair.*

MISS HETTY: Ah, Mr. Buchanan, I dozed off as the birds began to sing and left you neglected.

*It is true, the window has begun to brighten with morning.* MISS HETTY *lifts blankets, turns* BUCHANAN *over, holds bedpan unseen. He whimpers in pain. Instead of the sound of urination, silence. At last he cries:* I cannot!

*Offstage, a doorbell jangles.*

MISS HETTY (*impatient, holding bedpan*): Where is that nigger child? Never here when you need her. (*bells again*) That must be Mr. Swarr. (*goes out*)

BUCHANAN (*alone*): Heavenly Father, in the vast ledgers of Thy expenditure, let my accounts be said to balance, with some small deficit to be made up in the life to come. Let any flaw be mended amid the inflexible stars. Carry me through this. Be merciful to those of the earth who must survive. (*Pain strikes him.*) Ah! Doucement. Forgive me. Amen.

SWARR *enters. He is the* DOUGLAS *actor, in a Mennonite-style beard, with prim bald lips. In him the vein of blackness has become companionable to* BUCHANAN's *diaphanous, asymmetric pallor. He carries papers.*

SWARR (*sitting down at the bedside emphatically*): How goes the battle, Buck?

BUCHANAN: It goes, Hiram. It goes.

SWARR: You wanted to go over the will.

BUCHANAN: Yes. First, the trust for the Pleasanton sisters. My suspicion is, the Tioga Railroad stocks are presently inflated, and should be sold.

SWARR: And how about Hazleton Coal?

BUCHANAN: Do not sell. The earth . . . the earth is sound.

SWARR: Do you still adhere to the sixth clause? It may give rise to sarcasm.

BUCHANAN: Read it to me.

SWARR: "I give and bequeath to the city of Lancaster my two certificates of loan, Numbers forty-two and forty-three, from the said city, for one thousand dollars each, in trust to employ the annual interest of the same in purchasing fuel for the use of poor and indigent females of the city of Lancaster during the winter season. This bequest is to be incorporated with the fund of four thousand dollars provided by me some years ago for the same purpose and is to be administered in the same manner by the city authorities."

BUCHANAN: Let the louts on King Street laugh. A poor old hag or two, once a damsel, shall freeze a season later, thanks to James Buchanan.

SWARR: Are you satisfied that the clause excluding Johnston will not give offense?

BUCHANAN: Read it to me. Hiram, I cannot tell you the joy these clauses give me. My heart grows lighter with every one.

SWARR: "Whilst feeling full confidence in the integrity of Edward E. Johnston, husband of my niece Harriet Lane Johnston, I yet deem it prudent to secure to her a maintenance against the unforeseen contingencies of future years."

BUCHANAN: What reasonable man could take offense at that? I won't have this Baltimorean panjandrum squandering a dime that was mine. Insert, above, "full confidence in the integrity *and eminent business capacity* of Edward E. Johnston, et cetera." Now read me the sentence where I try to shield Miss Hetty from the avarice of my relatives.

SWARR (*searching*): ". . . Miss Esther Parker . . . five thousand . . . in addition to the two thousand already given to her she well deserves." Here. (*louder*) "I commend her to the kindness of all my relatives after my decease."

BUCHANAN (*laughs*): Oh, what a merry pack of great-nephews and -nieces I am engendering! No Sultan in his harem could be more abruptly fertile! Edward, he gets my clothes?

SWARR: "I give and bequeath to my brother, Edward Y. Buchanan, all my wearing apparel, my gold watch and seals."

BUCHANAN: Let him put on my Inaugural coat, see if he feels Hell's pinch in the armpits! Or let him strut before his wizened congregation in the black coat and pantaloons—"the simple dress of an American citizen"—in which I, with no more insignia than a black-hilted sword, dared present myself for audience before the Queen of half the planet. The ambassadors of all the courts of Europe held their breaths aghast, until Victoria smiled. Take it all, Edward, though it was my *skin* you burned to occupy!

SWARR: Maybe you should rest.

BUCHANAN: In a little, Hiram, I must. Have we remembered to deduct, from Harriet's share of all that is mine, the twelve thousand dollars for Wheatland itself?

SWARR: The provision is here.

BUCHANAN: She was high-spirited, you know, and women with high spirits must be restrained, lest they fling themselves headlong into the abyss. Their own lives are secondary to them, amidst the fevered stratagems of romance.

SWARR: I'll tell Mrs. Swarr to be careful.

BUCHANAN: You are ironical; forgive me. I grow lightheaded. Let us be solid men together. The stone. Is it absolutely clear?

SWARR: Durable white marble, bearing your name, your dates, and the words, "Fifteenth President of the United States."

BUCHANAN: Exactly. No more. "On parle peu, quand la vanité ne fait pas parler." Let me translate for you. "One says little, when vanity, oh, when vanity no longer goads us."

SWARR: Reverend Nevin, and I know Mrs. Johnston, wondered about a Biblical verse.

BUCHANAN: The Bible for Heaven; the Constitution for Earth. Let my stone be marred by facts beyond dispute. My name was such; I was born on such a day, and died on another; I was the fifteenth President of the United States. By this handle the fingers of God can pluck me from all eternity. It is enough; it is strange enough; it is glory enough. From many better men a fate so unambiguous has been withheld.

SWARR: Also Nevin asked about the Masons.

BUCHANAN: Let their mummery proceed. It was through the Masons that I began my climb; at the end of it the Masons stood guard at my door. But let their pomp be the only such display. No parades, no public travesty of grief. The harsh fact is, we rejoice at the death of others; "la ruine du prochain plaît aux amis et aux ennemis."

SWARR: The country people must be allowed to come; the little people. They love you.

BUCHANAN: Yes, as well they should; I tried to forestall magnificent events, on their behalf.

SWARR: And Mrs. Johnston had hoped, you might have some final words for the nation. It grieves her, that you are so much maligned.

BUCHANAN: She is impatient. Posterity will do me justice. I have always felt, and still feel, that I discharged every duty imposed on me conscientiously. I have no regret for any public act of my life; and history will vindicate my memory from every unjust aspersion.

SWARR: I will remember those words.

BUCHANAN: Between us—history is no great moralizer. Morality, I have come to feel, is a child of life, and moral indignation a tool of survival. Once death has equalized all men, worth flies from their deeds as utility flies from their artifacts. Are you leaving? Is it late?

SWARR: It is early.

BUCHANAN: Tell dear Harriet, lest she grieve herself about my reputation: "La mérite des hommes a sa saison aussi bien que les fruits." I die in a growing season. (*Turns his head; the window now is so full of light we see the gray limbs of a large beech tree in fresh leaf.*) "La fin du bien est un mal; la fin du mal est un bien."

SWARR: Now let's be quiet a while.

*They are quiet:* SWARR *sits,* BUCHANAN *moves in pain.*

BUCHANAN: I am rising like a bubble toward the light. (*laughs*) I see it. Légèreté. I rose *because* I was empty. Like a bubble in dark water, I rose. (*His body grows tense; he is in pain, and in another world.*) Ah! All that is heavy is fallen away.

SWARR (*calls*): Miss Hetty.

MISS HETTY *comes in, adjusts* BUCHANAN *on the bed. As she bends over, he says in her ear:* O Lord, God Almighty, as Thou wilt!

MISS HETTY *and* SWARR *sit and wait.* BUCHANAN's *breathing becomes amplified in the silence. A minute of this. His breathing, slower, merges, each breath, with a ring of his* BELL. *His breathing stops. The ringing continues one beat more. Silence. Curtain.*

# AFTERWORD

*Acknowledgments*

My main text, source, and guide has been *President James Buchanan*, by Philip Shriver Klein (University Park, Pa., 1962). In portraying the long, laborious life of this rather ubiquitous yet scarcely visible American politician, Professor Klein shows exemplary powers of research and sympathetic explication—powers earlier displayed in his *Pennsylvania Politics 1817–1832: A Game Without Rules* (Philadelphia, 1940). Without constant recourse to his biography I could never have realized my long-deferred hope of basing an imaginative composition of some kind upon the career of Pennsylvania's only successful aspirant to the White House. Indeed, my original intention of writing a novel was balked, in part, by the many novelistic touches with which Professor Klein animates his scholarly work. It is his happy idea, for instance, to begin the life with a prologue showing, on June 28, 1863, the old, calumniated ex-President waiting at Wheatland to see if the Confederate troops under Lee will cross the Susquehanna and sweep into Lancaster, where they might likely have taken Buchanan prisoner, if not slain him; certainly they would have razed his famous mansion, for, if much of the North viewed him as a Judas, the South did too, with better reason. As (in Klein's imagination) refugees flee east along the Marietta Pike, word arrives to the old man walking on his lawn that the Southern troops have been halted by the burning of the Columbia–Wrightsville bridge: "Nearly half a century before, while trying to save that bridge in a law court, he had lost Ann Coleman." Extending the symbol, the historian writes on: "Through all his later years, eschewing domesticity for politics, he had labored to keep strong the bridge of understanding and mutual regard between people of the North

: 151 :

and the South. The bridge was burning now, ruined as completely as his own life's work."

At the significant moment when Buchanan sails homeward from his mission in England toward his Presidential destiny, Klein sketches us a delightful Cruikshank:

> The steamship *Arago* slipped her cables and edged slowly out of her dock on noon on Wednesday, April 9, 1856. By midafternoon Buchanan had affably acknowledged the greetings of many of his fellow passengers, finished his constitutional around the deck, and retired to his stateroom where he took off his greatcoat, removed his cutaway, and then opened his travel chest to get his old leather slippers and a bottle of Madeira. After some puttering around he found the cork puller and a glass, lit a "segar" and then settled back on his bed, drew a long sigh of solid comfort, and relaxed.

At another egressive juncture, the young Buchanan's departure from Lancaster after the death of his fiancée, we are allowed to witness gestures unwitnessed in reality:

> A few days after the funeral, James Buchanan stepped from the rear door of his quarters into the gloomy morning darkness of December, made his way carefully across the cobblestone courtyard back of the Leopard Tavern, passed under the stone archway which led out to Duke Street, and there climbed aboard the early stage for the West. Huddled in his greatcoat, he made no effort to lean forward when the coach passed by the St. James churchyard. . . . Buchanan shivered from more than the cold, and let his thoughts merge with the bleak greyness of the winter dawn.

With such an intimate reconstruction already in print, there seemed little the fictionist could do but seek another form for the re-ordering of circumstance.

I am additionally in Professor Klein's debt for the several generous letters he wrote in response to my inquiries, and for sharing with me his speculations regarding the shadowy matter of Anne Coleman's death, beyond those presented in his article "James Buchanan and Ann Coleman" (*Lancaster County Historical Society Journal*, Vol. LIX, No. 1, 1955). What is known is this: late in November 1819, most probably on the immediate provocation of Buchanan's visit to the Hubley sisters, Anne wrote him a letter breaking off their engagement, which had been contracted that summer. On Saturday, December 4, with her younger sister Sarah, she went to Philadelphia, to visit with her sister Margaret, wife of Judge Hemphill. Buchanan stayed in Lancaster and on Monday, December 6, succeeded in getting an out-of-court settlement of the Columbia Bridge Company case. Early Thursday morning, a messenger brought the news to Lancaster that Anne Coleman had died at her sister's home shortly after midnight. That day, Judge Thomas Kittera of Philadelphia, a friend of the Colemans, wrote in his diary:

> At noon yesterday, I met this young lady on the street, in the vigour of health, and but a few hours after[,] her friends were mourning her death. She had been engaged to be married, and some unpleasant misunderstanding occurring, the match was broken off. This circumstance was preying on her mind. In the afternoon she was laboring under a fit of hysterics; in the evening she was so little indisposed that her sister visited the theatre. After night she was attacked with strong hysterical convulsions, which in-

duced the family to send for physicians, who thought this
would soon go off, as it did; but her pulse gradually weak-
ened until midnight, when she died. Dr. Chapman, who
spoke with Dr. Physick [*sic*], says it is the first instance he
ever knew of hysteria producing death. To affectionate parents sixty miles off what dreadful intelligence—to a younger
sister whose evening was spent in mirth and folly, what a
lesson of wisdom does it teach. Beloved and admired by all
who knew her, in the prime of life, with all the advantages
of education, beauty and wealth, in a moment she has been
cut off.[1]

The Kittera diary entry composes the main source of contemporary light on the incident. A letter from Hannah Cochran, of Lancaster, to her husband, written on December 14,
1819, states that town rumor had long accused Buchanan of
loving the Coleman fortune more than Anne, that after Anne
broke the engagement "her Mother persuaded her to go to
Philadelphia hoping that would ease her depressed spirits,"
and that after her death "her friends now look upon him as
her Murderer." A letter from Samuel Dale to Jacob Hibshman,
dated December 16, adds the information that Anne's vitality
was low and that she caught cold on the way to Philadelphia.
The letter (written December 10) from Buchanan to Robert
Coleman, read aloud by Coleman in my play, was returned
unopened, and survived accidentally, among Buchanan's general papers. Anne's letters, his own if she returned them, and
various relics of the affair were bundled up by Buchanan into
a package he cared so much about he sent it to a place of safe

---

[1]Extract from Kittera diary in notes of George Ticknor Curtis, Buchanan Papers, Historical Society of Pennsylvania. Quoted by Klein in article cited above.

deposit in New York City when, nearly half a century later, invasion threatened Lancaster. After his death, his executors found these papers with a note directing that they be destroyed without being read. Alas, the injunction was obeyed. However, George Ticknor Curtis, hired by Buchanan's executors and surviving relatives (Harriet Lane Johnston foremost) to compose a biography, knew a fuller story than he told; his account, meant for inclusion in the two-volume *Life* (1883), was submitted to Samuel L. M. Barlow, his friend and Buchanan's, for approval. Barlow replied: "I am clearly of the opinion that you should not print any considerable portion of what you have written on the subject of his engagement to Miss Coleman.... In this view Mrs. Barlow agrees fully." Curtis meekly acceded, and contented himself with these teasing sentences:

> It is now known that the separation of the lovers originated in a misunderstanding, on the part of the lady, of a very small matter, exaggerated by giddy and indiscreet tongues, working on a peculiarly sensitive nature. Such a separation, the commonest of occurrences, would have ended, in the ordinary course, in reconciliation, when the parties met, if death had not suddenly snatched away one of the sufferers, and left the other to a life-long grief.[2]

His confidence that the "lovers" would have been reunited may be rhetorical, or may have a basis in the information he did not disclose. The last authentic clue came years after the event, in an article written by Blanche Nevin, a niece of Grace Hubley. She wrote,

---

[2] Curtis, *Life of James Buchanan*, Vol. 1, p. 21.

Some time after the engagement had been announced, Mr. Buchanan was obliged to go out of town on a business trip. He returned in a few days and casually dropped in to see . . . Mrs. William Jenkins, with whose husband he was on terms of intimate friendship. With her was staying her sister, Miss Grace Hubley, . . . a pretty and charming young lady. From this innocent call the whole trouble arose. A young lady told Miss Coleman of it and thereby excited her jealousy. She was indignant that he should visit anyone before coming to her. On the spur of the moment she penned an angry note and released him from his engagement. The note was handed to him while he was in the Court House. Persons who saw him receive it remarked afterward that they noticed him turn pale when he read it. Mr. Buchanan was a proud man. The large fortune of his lady was to him only another barrier to his trying to persuade her to reconsider her rejection of himself.[3]

The letter that made him turn pale has, of course, been lost. The letter read in the play, in place of the indignant response of the South Carolina "Commissioners" (itself lost), is as much a fabrication as her conversation, though as harmonious as I can make it with what can be construed of her character, and of Buchanan's.

---

[3] Preserved, undated, in a scrapbook kept by John Lowry Ruth, of York, Pennsylvania. Quoted by Professor Klein in "James Buchanan and Ann Coleman." The ellipses are Klein's, not mine. Miss Nevin was the niece of the Reverend John W. Nevin who preached Buchanan's funeral sermon. A small world, Lancaster: William Jenkins, nine years after his wife had with such unfortunate consequences entertained the young lawyer in their home on Centre Square, built the orange-brick mansion "modeled after a French plan of the latter part of the Eighteenth Century" and named, for its view of grain fields, "The Wheatlands." Buchanan bought it from a subsequent owner in 1848. Now, handsomely restored, "Wheatland" is a national shrine, and houses on its grounds the Lancaster Historical Society.

The one document remaining to be mentioned is the obituary for Anne that appeared in the Lancaster *Journal* of December 11, 1819. Tradition has ascribed it to the pen of Buchanan himself, but a printer's devil sent for the copy reportedly found Buchanan "so disturbed by grief that he was unable to write the notice." Klein thinks Judge Walter Franklin (the same whose case brought Buchanan first fame) wrote it. Yet a lover's hyperbole does seem tenderly to stretch the terms of conventional eulogy:

> She was everything which the fondest parent or fondest friend could have wished her to be. Although she was young and beautiful, and accomplished, and the smiles of fortune shone upon her, yet her native modesty and worth made her unconscious of her own attractions. Her heart was the seat of all the softer virtues which ennoble and dignify the character of woman. . . . May the memory of her virtues be ever green in the hearts of her surviving friends.[4]

Whoever the author, the subject's name is given as "Anne," and this is the spelling I have preferred.

The affair fueled gossip and yellow journalism for the rest of Buchanan's life. Had the package of his keepsakes been preserved, they would illuminate, I believe, the details of the quarrel but not the central mystery: Did Anne commit suicide? Attempted suicide by taking laudanum was common in the time, but then so was sudden death from natural causes. Samuel Dale's mention of her cold supports the latter conjecture; the sixty-mile carriage ride to Philadelphia was grueling even for one not in "depressed spirits." But Hannah Cochran's use of the word "Murderer," Judge Kittera's glimpse of

---

[4]Quoted in Curtis's *Life*, Vol. 1, p. 18.

her "vigour of health," Dr. Chapman's puzzled (or conceal-
ing) diagnosis of "hysteria producing death," and the intense
aura of shame and horror that clung to Buchanan and that
seemed to Hannah Cochran certain to "lesson his Consequence in Lancaster," all suggest the darker possibility. As if
to corroborate suspicions of a willed death, a startling dupli-
cation of pattern arose six years later. Sarah Coleman, her
older sister's companion on the fatal excursion, had fallen in
love with the Reverend William Augustus Muhlenberg, rec-
tor of St. James's Church, wherein the Colemans were prom-
inent. Robert Coleman disputed a liturgical innovation the
young clergyman imposed and resisted his courtship of Sarah
more openly than ever he had Buchanan's of Anne. He for-
bade Muhlenberg to enter his house and wrote into his will a
proviso specifying that Sarah's inheritance of $50,000 was not
to be accessible to her husband if she married. Coleman died
in August of 1825; shortly after his will became public knowledge, Sarah abruptly fled to Philadelphia, and died there as
mysteriously as her sister, and at the very same age of twenty-
three.

From Washington in the late summer of 1856, when Buchanan's impending election to the Presidency had revived
gossip about him, Leonora Clayton wrote to Mary Ann Cobb
a succinct version of received rumor, with a hint of Coleman
authentication:

There is a cousin of his lady love residing here—a Miss
Coleman—and I have heard the family bear him no good
will, dating from that event. The story I heard—the lady
committed suicide in a fit of jealousy, believing he had
ceased to love her.[5]

---

[5] August 9, 1856. Cobb Papers, on deposit at the University of Georgia.

This is the version I have accepted and tried to dramatize.
Other possibilities of course exist. Perhaps Anne Coleman
was killed by the mixture of medicines given her by the attending physician, Dr. Chapman. He, the following year, in a
lecture on poisons, cited two cases in which, the previous
year, he had administered laudanum and an emetic to patients
who had swiftly died. However, both patients were also
"under the influence of alcohol," which does not seem likely
of Anne. Yet that many patients in this era were dispatched
not by the disease but by the treatment is beyond doubting; it
was common practice to bleed, purge, give an emetic and
then, to cap the ordeal, a sedative. Or perhaps, as her father in
Act III suggests, Anne was pregnant—a hypothesis that has
had its supporters and that would give her desperation a real
basis. But in the farm country of southeastern Pennsylvania as
I remember it, pregnancy did not disrupt engagements, it
hastened marriages. Anne and Buchanan were, after all, publicly betrothed; a sudden wedding would have been a harm-
less scandal. Our rural ancestors could become hysterical over
many things—comets and damnation, for two—but seldom
over fertility. In my estimation of the social and ethical condition of this prosperous and proper young couple, they would
not have had sexual intercourse nor, if another life *were* kin-
dled within her, would Anne have behaved self-destructively.
I imagine her as a suicide, but of the type that half-means it,
that in the innocence of egoism thinks to extend a living dialogue through death, and to force a rescue. Buchanan did
carry to his grave a guilty, solicitous feeling about the female
sex. Klein says, "it was a common joke during his presidency
(borne out by fact) that the way to get a political favor was to
send a woman with a hard-luck story to the White House."
But his original sin had to do, my guess is, less with lust than
with its opposite, what Roy Nichols, in his *Disruption of*

*American Democracy*, terms Buchanan's "inability to return affection adequately." Though this is vague, Nichols seems right when he says that Buchanan subsequently used Anne as a "romantic legend" "to shield himself": "He instinctively desired the world to sympathize with him as he loyally cherished the tender memory of a cruelly blighted love. Ever after, he had the ill equipped bachelor's eagerness for feminine attention to hide his peculiar lack, and he quite shone in the drawing room."[6]

The few certainties, with some attendant wisps of speculation, have been set forth so the reader can distinguish the facts within my fiction. In this, the central mystery of Buchanan's life, as where the sun of history beats glaringly down, I have sought to be the servant of what is known. In my play, the numerous Cabinet meetings of December 1860 have been necessarily telescoped; a surreal imp entered the dialogue whenever Harriet Lane came onstage; and I mistakenly transposed the meeting of Buchanan and Susan Keitt to the wrong winter, and let the mistake stand. Otherwise, the historical record has not been knowingly distorted or skimped. In more details than could be listed, Professor Klein's account of both Buchanan's psychology and his politics has guided me. Especially did I borrow from his analysis of Buchanan's reasoning on Lecompton and the action, or lack of it, during the fraught four months between Lincoln's election and inauguration; Klein's relation of Buchanan's wavering Sumter course to other events (Howell Cobb's resignation, Lincoln's own wavering in Springfield) seemed notably subtle and original. Indeed, Klein makes a more vigorous case for Buchanan than the former President himself did, in his *Mr. Buchanan's Administration on the Eve of the Rebellion* (1865).

---

[6]Nichols, *Disruption*, p. 88.

However great my debt to others, my mistakes are all my own. Professor Klein has never seen my curious manuscript, nor have I ever exploited his kind willingness to suffer an interview. I wanted to seize Buchanan's life so as to apprehend its shape—his "fate"—with my own hands. In his first letter to me (September 10, 1968), with a beautiful solicitude for the dead, Professor Klein expressed his fear that Buchanan, "who in his lifetime and later received an incredibly cruel hatcheting," would be subjected again to "the old character assassination bit." He hoped that was not my intention, adding, "A real character study would be fine." Without presuming that my product will strike him as fine, I hope the professor will see how far my intentions were from any denigration of our hero.

The other books devoted mainly to Buchanan are few:

*Life of James Buchanan*, by George Ticknor Curtis, in two volumes (New York, 1883). Curtis (1812–1894) was a New Englander, Harvard graduate, lawyer, and authority on constitutional history who turned to writing—a biography of Daniel Webster and a pseudonymous novel are among his other compositions. He had defended Dred Scott and was the brother of Supreme Court Justice Benjamin R. Curtis, but had had no extensive personal acquaintance with Buchanan. He was approached by the family after Buchanan's chosen confidant, James F. Shunk, then his friend William B. Reed, and finally Judge John Cadwallader had all proved unequal to the task of writing the biography of a public figure excoriated as a weakling, if not a traitor, for decades after the Civil War. Curtis, though his preface disavows the eulogist's role, was by disposition polite (as his suppression of the Coleman facts shows) and by training equipped to understand little but the legal niceties of Buchanan's position—

which of course fitted him well to expound his subject's version of events. Buchanan, in the years of his retirement, had not only written his own *apologia* but had assembled many of his papers and letters; through the thirteen hundred pages of his two volumes, Curtis quotes extensively from these. He even includes such items as Buchanan's annual income in the years of legal practice:

$$
\begin{array}{ll}
1813 & \$938 \\
1814 & \$1,096 \\
1815 & \$2,246 \\
1816 & \$3,174 \\
1817 & \$5,379 \\
1818 & \$7,915 \\
1819 & \$7,092 \\
1820 & \$5,665 \\
\end{array}
$$

Whatever else Anne Coleman's death did to Buchanan, it only slightly affected his earning capacity.

Curtis, though his ceremonious style can be quaint, was much closer in time to Buchanan than we, and his stiff pages brush up against the man in a way no modern analysis can. Many of Buchanan's intimates were still living, and Curtis talked or corresponded with them. From Barlow, for instance, he heard that Buchanan in London had confided his strange (and typically forked) reason for entering politics in 1820: "As a distraction from my great grief, and because I saw that through a political following I could secure the friends I then needed, I accepted a nomination." From Buchanan's nephew and secretary, James Buchanan Henry, Curtis obtained a long and valuable reminiscence of his uncle, and from the Reverend William Paxton a letter describing the remarkable interview at Bedford Springs in August of 1860; in my scene of this episode, I have taken the beginning and the end of the conversation just as Reverend Paxton gave them. The middle, I had to invent. Buchanan's type of scrupulous self-scrutiny and religious uncertainty was not uncommon; Howell Cobb, for one, also went to church conscientiously, yet suffered persistent doubts as to his election. A post-Freudian man, perhaps, similarly anguishes over his sexual effectiveness.

*James Buchanan and His Cabinet on the Eve of Secession*, by Philip Gerald Auchampaugh (privately printed in Lancaster, Pa., 1926). Auchampaugh is the principal Buchananian between Curtis and Klein. His piecing together, from numerous contemporary accounts and later reminiscences, the conflicting and heightened versions of what went on in the White House in the last four months of Buchanan's administration is well researched, fascinating, sometimes flossily written, and aggressively pro-Buchanan. Conversations within the Cabinet are given at greater length than in Klein, and Southern sources such as Floyd's diary and Thompson's letters to the Philadelphia *Press* are consulted as well as the self-promoting memoirs of Stanton and Black. Black, indeed, rendered several scenarios of his dramatic Sunday morning interview with the President, and I regret not being able to find a place in my dialogue for his sartorial image, "I promised that as long as there was a button to the coat I would cling to it."[7]

Auchampaugh also published, in *Tyler's Quarterly Historical and Genealogical Magazine* (Nos. 3 and 4, January and April 1939), a two-part article entitled "James Buchanan, the Bachelor of the White House: An Inquiry On the Subject of Feminine Influence in the Life of Our Fifteenth President."

---

[7]Philadelphia *Press*, September 10, 1883, as told to Col. Frank Burr.

Among the ladies in his life with which Buchanan is *not* taunted in Act III are the widowed Mrs. Polk and the plebeian Mary Sherry, whose account of her attendance upon Buchanan in his last illness became mysteriously transmuted into my apparition of Ann Cook.[8] Auchampaugh also has much lively to say of Harriet Lane—"Miss Lane did not have in her youth the bland spirit of her uncle James. Oh, no, there was much more fire and flame in her disposition." He quotes the cloying "Ladies of the White House," by Laura C. Holloway:

> Although Mr. Buchanan was not particularly fond of children, he was attracted to this frank and handsome child from her earliest infancy . . . No doubt that even at that early age he recognized in her a kindred spirit, and his good angel whispered to him that the boisterous child who sometimes disturbed his studies and mimicked his best friends, would one day be to him a fit adviser in difficulty, a sympathetic companion in sorrow, the light and ornament of his public life, and the comfort, at last, of his lonely hearth.

Mrs. Holloway perpetuates the sketch of Harriet's beauty written by a friend, a Miss Schomberg, who saw golden hair and violet irises where accountants less dazzled registered auburn and blue:

> Miss Lane was a blonde, with deep violet eyes, golden hair, classic features and bright expression, and a mouth of pecu-

---

[8] "'I gave him his last drink of water when he was dying,' she says, her eyes filling as the scenes of those days grow more vivid in her memory."—Lancaster *Sunday News*, June 3, 1928, interview with Mary Sherry.

liar beauty. Her form had a statuesque majesty, and every movement was grace.

It is regrettable that the surviving portraits of Harriet Lane show her either as a white-haired matron, elusively smooth, or, as done by Brady in her White House prime, forbiddingly stout and staring—more Volumnia than Rosalind. However, one of the earliest photographs taken of American leadership incidentally catches her in her youthful beauty. A recently discovered daguerreo-type (in the collection of Eastman House in Rochester, reproduced in *The American Heritage Pictorial History of the Presidents*) shows Polk—his eyes the lightless sockets of the soon-to-die—posed with some of his Cabinet and their ladies. On the extreme left edge of the exposure stands a tall dim figure with a sloping corporation— Secretary of State James Buchanan. Next to him, erect and lissom in a pale checked dress decked out with pleated flounces, her eyes downcast and her golden hair appearing black, is Harriet Lane, no more than fifteen years old. She stands out among the other ladies, bonneted and grim, like an Ingres among Copleys.

Auchampaugh's article includes one specimen of her wit, a remarkable retort that, if I mistake not, is naughty, rhymes, and rebukes her conversational partner all at once:

> Miss Lane was not only discreet, but, like her uncle, quick at repartee and clever in conversation. She had very beautiful hands, and many of her friends wish she had learned to play the harp because of them. She never learned, although she had a talent for music and played well on the piano. A young gentleman once warmly expressed the thought that her hands were fitted to play the harp or guide

the path of Empire. Quickly as a flash came the reply, "or awake to ecstasies the living lyre."

So perhaps the antic tone she brings to my stage is not so surreal after all.

*The Works of James Buchanan,* collected and edited by John Bassett Moore, in twelve volumes (New York, 1908–1911). Only in an eternal Hell could one read through this shelf of congressional speeches, diplomatic dispatches, Presidential papers, and letters political and personal. The letters to Harriet and the letters from Russia (1832–1833) are revealing and amusing, however. Volume XII contains Buchanan's book in his own defense; a spirited address along the same lines (and with an oddly identical title) given by W. U. Hensel to the Cliosophic Society of Lancaster on January 24, 1908; the autobiographical fragment (1791–1828) that Buchanan had composed at an uncertain date, possibly to assist R. G. Horton in the preparation of his campaign biography of 1856; the opening part of the Fourth of July speech of 1815, which had turned up since the speech's second half had been printed in Volume I; a biographical sketch prepared by James Buchanan Henry for Curtis but only quoted in part in Curtis's *Life*; and a letter from Henry to Moore refuting a "*ludicrous* error" in Von Holst's *Constitutional History of the United States.* Moore carried out his Herculean task with admirable care, faithfully reproducing Buchanan's punctuation and liberal use of ampersands, bemoaning in several instances Curtis's carelessness in printing the same material. Moore also, in his introduction, gives about as good a one-sentence summary of Buchanan's Presidential predicament as can be given:

It was the fate of James Buchanan, in his seventieth year, when, at the close of a long and wearing public career, he was about to lay down the burdens of office, to be confronted with a crisis which would have taxed the energy and decision of an Andrew Jackson at thirty-five, and concerning the wisest treatment of which even the philosophers of hindsight cannot agree.

If Buchanan scholarship were in a thriving state, the *Works* could be supplemented by at least one volume of Buchanan letters to which Moore had no access. In the Cobb papers at the University of Georgia, for instance, I found two to Howell Cobb, one advising him to stay away from dinner at the White House, since Robert Walker was coming,[9] and the other accepting Cobb's resignation.[10] Both letters are vintage Buchanan, in their somewhat wooden felicity. There are as well unpublished letters *to* Buchanan of interest— for instance, the Machiavellian ones written to him by Slidell

---

[9]"My dear Sir/
15 May 59

Robert J. Walker is to dine with me to day. When we meet I shall tell you all about it. Perhaps you had better dine with some other friend to day. In any event, you had better stay all night with us & start with me in the morning. Will you not come to me after Church & in the mean time say nothing about my guest for dinner.

Yr friend
always
J.B."

[10][dated 10 Dec. 1860] ". . . I deeply regret that you have determined to separate yourself from us at the present critical moment, yet I admit that the question was one for your own decision. I could have wished you had arrived at a different conclusion; because our relations both official & personal have been of the most friendly & confidential character. I may add that I have been entirely satisfied with the ability & zeal which you have displayed in performing the duties of your important office."

If the first note has the gaiety of flirtation, this second is a wounded lover's. In 1867, after Cobb had served the Confederacy in rather less exalted positions than he might have expected, he met Harriet in Baltimore, who wrote her uncle and asked if he wished to meet his old friend. Buchanan wrote back, "I do not wish to meet him now or hereafter. . . . I wish him well and hope he may obtain his pardon; but this is all. . . ." [quoted in Klein, p. 426]

in the 1850's, kept at the Historical Society of Pennsylvania.[11]

*The Life and Public Services of James Buchanan*, by R. G. Horton (New York, 1856). A campaign biography consisting of speeches stuck together with laud. However, the pre-1857 perspective is vivifying; musty old issues like the tariff and specie payments walk around as if alive, and the sense of present contention animates the account of Buchanan's congressional career. The bias of praise is revealing; repeatedly Horton presents his candidate as "a model of consistency" [p. 138], even though "Where is the man, who in the period of forty years' experience in public life, has not changed?" [p. 29] The first chapter follows Buchanan's autobiographical

---

[11]A sample of Slidell's wisdom, from a letter dated 18 October 1854: "I always regretted the too easy victory of the last presidential campaign. a strong minority is always necessary to the preservation of harmony & discipline in the ranks of the majority, we wanted the wholesome pressure from without so indispensable to sound party organization. The lesson is a severe one, but its ultimate effects will be salutary if we have sufficient discretion to make the proper use of it." Discretion, indeed, is what the two friends were always urging upon each other. In a letter written as Secretary of State, Buchanan orders Slidell, on a secret mission to Mexico, to tell the dictator, Paredes, "in some discreet manner that the U.S. were both able and willing to relieve his administration from pecuniary embarrassment." A decade later, when Buchanan was ambassador in London, Slidell advises him to indicate his willingness to accept the Presidential nomination "to some *discreet* friend or friends." Of himself Slidell said, "a strong will with some tact and discretion can affect a great deal." These last three quotations are from *John Slidell*, by Louis Martin Sears (Durham, 1925), which does draw upon the Buchanan repository at Philadelphia. Two more examples of working discretion quoted in this biography: Slidell, advising Buchanan not to seek the governorship of Pennsylvania: ". . . you should not voluntarily place yourself in a position where you will be called upon to express your opinions on the subject of slavery in the territories . . . you see I have not lost my hopes of yet seeing you in the White House" [15 July 1849]. And, to Buchanan abroad, in the same letter of 18 October 1854: "Is it true that you intend returning to the United States next summer? allow me to advise that unless you have insurmountable objections to a more protracted stay in Europe, you should reconsider this decision, the political atmosphere is malarious (if there be no such word there should be) & those who are not compelled to inhale it had better keep away." However, with the Presidency assured, Slidell predicted, "You are not to lie in a bed of roses for the next four years . . ."

sketch, with suitable inflation, and from the stock of contemporary myth furnishes an image of him at striking variance with that of the feeble and fussy old Public Functionary.

At this period of his life, Mr Buchanan was tall, slender, and graceful. He had been cradled in poverty, and at all times inured to hardships and toil. He exercised much in the open air, and the forests of Pennsylvania often resounded with the crack of the rifle of the young sportsman, who, at an early age, like nearly all Americans, learned how to use this sharp-shooting weapon. So dexterous was he with his rifle, that like a true back-woods-man, he considered it a disgrace to go home with squirrels or similar game, unless the ball had been sent with unerring precision directly through the head. His studies had expanded his mind, while his labors and recreations had given strength to his body, and already laid the firm foundation for a long life of uniform health. There can be no doubt that his vigorous, early training has been the means of giving him that wonderful endurance, which so remarkably distinguished him in after-life as a public man. The amount of labor he can perform is perfectly astonishing, and has always been remarked by all who have known him, both while engaged in his profession and in his duties in Congress.

Four hundred pages later, the same note of vigor is sounded: "Such is the man now presented to the American people for their suffrages. In the sunset of an honorable life, with his eye yet undimmed, and his natural force unabated, he is brought forward by the spontaneous voice of his countrymen."

In the matter of general antebellum history, my first move, a bold one, was to ask guidance from Professor Henry Steele

Commager, on the excuse of a fascinating incomplete sentence in an article in the *New Republic* of July 6, 1968. The sentence enigmatically read: "Buchanan probably knew more about American politics than any other occupant of the White House, but in the judgement of historians." Professor Commager wrote back that the sentence should have continued with the words, *"was by universal consent the worst President in the history of the country."* And, low as this opinion was, he kindly provided me, from I assume the resources of his memory, with an excellent bibliography on Buchanan and his era, which I gratefully followed. ·

*The Emergence of Lincoln,* by Allan Nevins, in two volumes (New York, 1950). The title is misleading. In fact Nevins, marshalling an awesome richness of detail and quotation in a prose that never loses dramatic sweep and argumentative edge, covers the years 1857–1861, ranging from New England literature to California mining in a magisterial survey of events most of which had nothing to do with Lincoln. Lincoln's greatness, rather than slowly and logically emergent, comes as in the sentence of de Tocqueville: "Great characters are . . . thrown into relief, as edifices which are concealed by the gloom of night are illuminated by the glare of a conflagration." Of Buchanan, Nevins thinks he thoroughly botched Lecompton: "Seldom in the history of the nation has a President made so disastrous a blunder as Buchanan was about to commit." He brushes aside the awkward truth that "the Lecompton convention was quite legal," a minimization with which Klein, in one of his few direct challenges to another historian, takes bitter exception. Nevins' character sketch of Buchanan reaches the conventional verdict: "Of the same Scotch-Irish stock as Jackson, Calhoun, and Polk, he showed hardly a rusty fleck of the iron in these notable men." Yet with his admirable power to evoke historical figures in the round, Nevins shades his portrait interestingly:

> In a line of mediocre Presidents, not one of whom would be esteemed fit today to head a large corporation, bank, or university, he had more ability than Taylor or Fillmore, more steadiness than Pierce, and more civil experience than the three combined. Yet he was as ill-equipped for a supreme test as they. By half-measures, evasions, and stealthy approaches, by all the arts of weakness, he had gained the Presidency at just the moment when a man of all but superhuman vision and strength was needed.

In the "supreme test," however, Nevins does not find the old man altogether wanting. "The President was entirely right in determining upon a policy of peace, conciliation, and delay. This was the statesmanlike course, offering the one hope of preserving the Union without carnage, destruction, and hatred." His faults, it appears, were ones of execution—in the most detailed attempt I know of to pinpoint Buchanan's blunders in the secession winter, Nevins lists four, all of which amount to the same thing, a lack of Jacksonian vigor. He should have immediately delivered a "spirited appeal to national sentiment"; he should have fired Cobb and Thompson from the Cabinet; he should have reinforced the Charleston forts swiftly and made clear the government's willingness to fight over them; he should have pressed "with instant vigor" his plan for a national convention and bypassed the deadlocked politicians of the Congress. Both Nevins' first and fourth proposals involve rallying the people inspirationally to the dreary cause of compromise and forestallment, and I wonder how real this possibility was, in an age accustomed to a narrowly executive Presidency, before the electronic communications that made it possible for, say, a Franklin Roosevelt to rise high above the governmental machinery of Washington. As to Cobb and Thompson, Cobb soon left, and Thompson found himself helpless against Stanton, Black, Holt, and Buchanan. Reinforcement of the Charleston forts, when it came in April of 1861, brought war, as it would have months earlier: "Buchanan was unquestionably right in thinking that a military and naval demonstration against South Carolina in November of 1860 would have precipitated war." As it was, only Anderson's unpredictable failure to fire back when the *Star of the West* was shelled saved Buchanan from igniting the conflagration. His often-expressed desire to avoid firing the first shot was more, I think, than habitual timidity; it expressed his wise instinct that, in a democracy—as we have seen in the last decade—the people can only be rallied, and then totally, to a cause that is made to appear righteous. The South over decades had been goaded to self-righteousness; the North needed, perhaps, all these months of weakness and forbearingness in Washington to give a defensive coloring to the dubious cause of putting down secession with force. On November 9, 1860, Greeley had written in the *Tribune*, "Whenever a considerable section of our Union shall deliberately resolve to go out, we shall resist all coercive measures designed to keep it in." In fact, a nation is as little likely not to resist the loss of a section as is an animal not to resist the losing of a limb. But Buchanan's much-derided speech of December 3rd correctly located a silence in the Constitution; nowhere in it is a State forbidden to withdraw from the Union. (He rather prettily argues that the phrase in the preamble, "to form a perfect union," necessarily includes in its increased perfection the "essential attribute of perpetuity" implicit in the phrase "confederation and perpetual union" used in the superseded Articles of Confederation.) Buchanan set the federal case the only place where it could stand: on the federal government's right to defend its property and enforce its laws against not States but citizens. Lincoln, Nevins admits, "came into power with a policy essentially identical."[12] When, after six more weeks of hold-off, the South Carolinians bombarded Sumter, Lincoln could draw upon the moral capital Buchanan's conciliation had piled up. "I appeal to all loyal citizens," his proclamation of war began, "to favor, facilitate and aid this effort to maintain the honor, the integrity, and the existence of our National Union . . . and to redress wrongs already long enough endured."

The account of the Dred Scott decision which Harriet Lane in Act III reads aloud as a news item is taken from Nevins, himself once a journalist.

*The Disruption of American Democracy*, by Roy Franklin Nichols (New York, 1948). Again, a misleading title— "Democracy" refers not to the nation as a whole but to what we now call the Democratic party. Nichols places the party "under the microscope," state machine by state machine, to arrive at a pluralistic analysis of the breakup, between the Northern/Douglas and Southern/Buchanan wings, of the co-

---

[12]Quotes from Nevins, in order given, found on pp. 239, 246, 61, and 64 of Volume I, and pp. 361, 341, and 380 of Volume II. Nevins elsewhere seems to argue against his own urging of Jacksonian dash upon Buchanan: "The main objective of Buchanan, the preservation of peace until compromise and sober second thought could bring the two sections together, was entirely sound. Most indices of public opinion suggest that the country desired caution, delay, and conciliation. A rough Jacksonian threat of force would have been repugnant to it. Buchanan believed that forbearance and moderation would keep the Upper South in the Union, that it would give time for placatory measures, and that the Lower South, finding itself alone and gradually softening under the offer of new guarantees, would return to its old allegiance. This was a reasonable policy." [Vol. II, p. 341]

hesive party of Jackson. Where Nevins in his conclusion blames the failure of American leadership to face "squarely" the "problem of slavery *with its complementary problem of race-adjustment,*" Nichols more fatalistically borrows a term from Machiavelli: the "confusion of a growing state." More particularly, "the war was the product of the chaotic lack of system in ascertaining and directing the public will, a chaos exploited with little regard for the welfare of the general public by irresponsible and blind operators of local political machinery unchecked by any adequate central organization." Nichols, a Pennsylvanian, has the patience of an amused Jove in tracing the ins and outs of political manipulation, and a vivifying love for the smell and feel of politicians at work. He emphasizes physical Washington—the malarious climate, the stuffy Capitol chambers, the "mud and marble, fragrant magnolias and odoriferous Tiber," the booze and spittoons and bad plumbing—and his portrayal of Buchanan (already referred to) incorporates a medical history:

> He had been ill, off and on, for a decade. He had suffered from glandular difficulty in his neck and from polypus growths in the nasal passages, from which he had sought relief by submitting to the crude operative techniques of the day. He was also bothered by heart trouble which recent arduous diplomatic experiences in London had not helped. Now he was weakened by the National Hotel disease from which he recovered slowly. These physical handicaps accentuated his natural tendency to be indecisive and even timid.

In line with this diagnosis Nichols asserts that Buchanan became hysterically addled by the events of December 1860:

The President, who only a few days before had boasted of a calm spirit, was now nervous and hysterical. Justice Campbell thought him completely unmanned, with his mind having lost its power of comprehending a complicated situation. The course of events certainly had endorsed Campbell's opinion.[13]

While the stresses of this crisis undoubtedly wore at the old gentleman (Mrs. W. M. Gwin wrote to Mary Ann Cobb on January 5, 1861, "He looks badly. His face indicates much unhappiness & when I see him I feel like comforting him, but you know him well enough to know no one could approach him in that way"), in the course of events Buchanan with his reorganized Cabinet evolved a policy that held until the end of his administration; he courageously performed the far-from-traditional courtesy of riding with the President-elect to the inauguration platform; and he lived for seven more years. Truly, as I have him say, "tougher than they thought."

Then there are three "coming" books:

*The Coming Fury*, by Bruce Catton, 1961;

*The Coming of the Civil War*, by Avery Craven (3rd edn., 1966);

*And the War Came*, by Kenneth M. Stampp, 1950. Catton, who has all of Nevins' color but not his gravity ushers Buchanan out of the White House almost with a commendation: "He was turning over the government to Lincoln without having made a single admission of the right of secession and without having committed Lincoln to hold even an informal conversation with the commissioners from Montgomery. The border slave states were still in the Union. An-

---

[13]Nichols, *Disruption*, pp. 8, 502, 505, 17, 89, 424.

derson was still in Fort Sumter (even though his dispatch, read this morning, indicated he could not possibly stay there much longer), and Buchanan had firmly asserted the Federal government's right to keep him there. All in all, the departing President felt he had not done too badly."[14] Craven's purpose is a large one: to rescue the "three decades of bitter sectional strife" preceding the outbreak of war from history books written by the victors. He gives, then, a Southern point of view and an economic overview of early American history that includes a description of slavery as a "labor system." On a canvas of such breadth, the specific strokes devoted to Buchanan are curt and perhaps more decisive than the evidence warrants. "Buchanan then brought Greer [sic] into line, and the result was the famous Dred Scott decision . . ." "Studiously [Buchanan] avoided any act that might precipitate conflict. He was no Jackson and he knew it."[15] Stampp, examining Northern attitudes during the secession crisis, makes the point, in his chapter "A Doughface Chooses the Union," that Buchanan proved more of a Unionist than both his Yankee detractors and Southern friends might have expected.

What, then, was to be expected of this "doughface," this northern outcast, this ally of secessionists, when the Union was imperiled? Only that he would be the chief architect of national ruin, that he would climax his subservience to the

---

[14] Catton, *The Coming Fury*, p. 264.

[15] Craven, *The Coming of the Civil War*, pp. 383, 429. His controversially sympathetic discussion of slavery occupies pp. 67–93; it traces the rebirth of this "very ancient labor system" in America to its origins in indentured labor, relates the slave's condition to the generally laborious conditions of the new country, and quotes Edward Bryan's distinction, "Our slave property lies only *incidently* in the *person* of the slave; but *essentially* in his *labor*." For all this, however, Craven concludes, "The fact that it could be as bad as was possible where the worst white man could own the best Negro cancelled all that its defenders could say in its defense."

South by abdicating the executive power to aid the cause of rebellion. . . . Such, at least, was the forecast of a large segment of the northern press. . . . Yet, considering his southern sympathies, his state-rights proclivities, and his low reputation in the North, Buchanan's actual record in the secession crisis contains some significant surprises. Viewed retrospectively, his indictment falls rather flat. When the tug actually came, he quickly proved that he shared one basic concept with the nationalists: a deep belief in the perpetuity of the Union.[16]

All in all, I did not find in these general histories confirmation that Buchanan was "the worst President in the history of the country." That a few forts were seized while he vainly begged a compromise formula from the Congress does not seem to me significant, weighed against the irresistible mass of Union mobilization when open conflict finally came. Elected amid rising sectionalism to keep the peace for four more years, he performed the job for which he was hired. He ran foreign affairs with a competence few deny. In a domestic crisis of unmatched severity, he defined a minimal sticking point, and stuck with it through the worst personal battering any President had ever received in the performance of his duties. Needless to say, I am no historian. Nor does Buchanan's hypothetical ranking among the forty others who have held his office affect my attempt to make him live as a character in a narrative action (though it may be, in these years of high indignation over unbridled and corrupting Presidential power, that we can give more sympathy to Buchanan's cautious and literal constitutionalism than has been shown him

---

[16]Stampp, *And the War Came*, 47–8.

in history books written by Lincolnophiles and neo-abolitionists). I accept my character's reasoning on Lecompton and Sumter, but do feel that his antipathy toward Douglas (which played its part in the Southern intransigence at the Charleston convention that split the party and made Lincoln's victory certain) has in it something irrational, which my play offers to explain psychologically.

Other books read or consulted:

*Division and Reunion: 1829–1889*, by Woodrow Wilson, 1898.

*The Union Divides: Politics and Slavery, 1850–1861*, by Henry F. Bedford, 1963.

*The Nation Divided*, selected from *The American Reader*, by Paul M. Angle, 1960.

*The Civil War in America*, by Alan Barker, 1961.

*The American Heritage Short History of the Civil War*, by Bruce Catton, 1960.

*Reconstruction After the Civil War*, by John Hope Franklin, 1961.

*Slavery Attacked: The Abolitionist Crusade*, edited by John L. Thomas, 1965.

*Slavery Defended: The Views of the Old South*, edited by Eric L. McKitrick, 1963.

*The American Heritage Pictorial History of the Presidents*, Volume I, 1968.

*Sixteen American Presidents*, by David Bruce, 1953.

*George Washington: Man and Monument*, by Marcus Cunliffe, 1958.

*Andrew Jackson*, by Marquis James, 1937.

*The Diary of James K. Polk During His Presidency, 1845 to 1849* (four vols.), 1910.

*Franklin Pierce: Young Hickory of the Granite Hills*, by Roy F. Nichols, 1931.

*Abraham Lincoln*, by Carl Sandburg (three vols.), 1926–39.

*The Life, Correspondence, and Speeches of Henry Clay*, by Calvin Colton, 1864.

*John Slidell*, by Louis Martin Sears, 1925.

*The American Talleyrand*, by Holmes Alexander, 1935.

*Memoirs of John Quincy Adams*, publ. 1874–77.

*Jeremiah Sullivan Black*, by William Norwood Brigance, 1934.

*Stephen A. Douglas*, by Robert W. Johannsen, 1973.

*To Purge This Land with Blood: A Biography of John Brown*, by Stephen B. Oates, 1970.

*Stanton*, by Benjamin Platt Thomas and Harold Melvin Hyman, 1962.

*American Secretaries of State and Their Diplomacy*, edited by Samuel Flagg Bemis, Volume VI, 1928: articles on "Lewis Cass" by Lewis Einstein and "Jeremiah Sullivan Black" by Roy F. Nichols.

*Twelve American Ambassadors* (USIS, London), 1961.

*America's Ambassadors to England (1786–1928)*, by Beckles Willson, 1928.

*Russo-American Relations, 1815–1867*, by Benjamin Platt Thomas, 1930.

*Eight Years in Congress, from 1857–1865*, by Samuel S. Cox, 1865.

*The Stakes of Power, 1845–1877*, by Roy F. Nichols, 1961.

*Trimmers, Trucklers, & Temporizers*, notes of Murat Halstead from the Political Conventions of 1856, edited by William B. Hesseltine and Rex. G. Fisher, 1961.

*Three Against Lincoln*, by Murat Halstead, edited by William B. Hesseltine, 1960.

*The Great Secession Winter and Other Essays*, by Henry Adams, edited by George Hochfield, 1958.

*Letters of Henry Adams (1858–1891)*, edited by Worthington Chauncy Ford, 1930.

*Recollections of a Busy Life*, by Horace Greeley, 1868.

*Letters from Europe*, by John W. Forney, 1867.

*Forty Years of American Journalism; Retirement of Mr. J. W. Forney from the Philadelphia "Press,"* 1877.

*Seventy-Five Years of White House Gossip*, by Edna M. Colman, 1925.

*First First Ladies, 1789–1865*, by Mary Ormsbee Whitton, 1948.

*Old Lancaster*, by Frederick Shriver Klein, 1964.

*The Covode Investigation* (36th Congress, 1st Session, Report No. 648), 1860.

*Evening Exercises for the Closet: For Every Day in the Year*, by William Jay, 1832.

*Sentences et Maximes de Morale*, 1664; *Maxims*, by the Duc de La Rochefoucauld, translated by L. W. Tancock, 1959.


Some articles:

"The Narrative of William Henry Trescott," edited by C. H. Ambler, *American Historical Review*, XIII (April 1908).

"President James Buchanan's Betrayal of Governor James Walker of Kansas," by George D. Harmon, *Pennsylvania Magazine of History and Biography*, LIII (1929), 51–91.

"James Buchanan and Ann Coleman," by Philip Shriver Klein, *Lancaster County Historical Society Journal*, LIX (1955), 1–20.

"Harriet Lane," by Ida L. K. Hofstetter, *LCHSJ*, XXXIII (1929), 97–112.

"John Forney, Journalist and Politician," by George R. Dowdell, *LCHSJ*, LV (1951), 49–66.

"Robert Coleman, Millionaire Ironmaster," by Frederick S. Klein, *LCHSJ*, LXIV (1960), 17–33.

"The Celebrated Mrs. Cobb," by Elizabeth Mays, *Georgia Historical Quarterly*, XXIV (March and June 1940).

I am grateful for permissions and courtesies granted me by staff members of the British Museum, the Library of Congress, and of the libraries of Harvard University, the University of Georgia, Duke University, the Historical Society of Pennsylvania, and the Lancaster County Historical Society. Specific points of information were kindly supplied by these scholars: Henry Steele Commager, Christopher Lasch, Leon Edel, Malcolm Cowley (who satisfied me that Faulkner never mentions his fellow-Oxonian Jacob Thompson, though Thompson's mansion was the most palatial in ante-bellum Oxford and the only residence burnt by the Union troops), José de Vinck.

And I am most grateful to Carole (Mrs. Richard D.) Sherr, of Leola, Pennsylvania: she volunteered to do Lancaster research for me and never faltered under my demands for petty information. Rather than have her hard work come to nothing, I persevered with this radically imperfect book.

*Buchanan Quotes*

Though Buchanan is one of the obscurer Presidents, quotations pertinent to him do strike the sensitized eye, and I was tempted to add to my opening set of five, but for destroying their symmetry,

The situation during all the administration of President Pierce was only less threatening and stormy than that under the administration of James Buchanan. One sowed, the other reaped. One was the wind, the other was the whirlwind.

—Frederick Douglass, in his *Life and Times*

All who know me, consider me an eminently *safe* man.

—Herman Melville, *Bartleby*

The course I followed, of regarding the Executive as subject only to the people, and, under the Constitution, bound to serve the people affirmatively in cases where the Constitution does not explicitly forbid him to render the service, was substantially the course followed by both Andrew Jackson and Abraham Lincoln. Other honorable and well-meaning Presidents, such as James Buchanan, took the opposite and, as it seems to me, narrowly legalistic view that the President is the servant of Congress rather than of the people, and can do nothing, no matter how necessary it be to act, unless the Constitution explicitly commands the action. Most able lawyers who are past middle age take this view, and so do large numbers of well-meaning, respectable citizens. My successor in office took this, the Buchanan, view of the President's powers and duties.

—Theodore Roosevelt, *Autobiography*[17]

---

[17]TR not infrequently cites Buchanan as a prime example of how not to be President. I wonder if he realized how much, in his policy toward Latin America, Buchanan wielded the "big stick"—"No President . . . until Theodore Roosevelt would propose so aggressive a policy in the Caribbean" [Klein, p. 317]. He diminished British influence in Central America, won transit rights from Nicaragua, sent a show of nineteen warships against remote Paraguay, and almost (the Senate failed to concur by a vote of thirty-one to twenty-five) established a protectorate over the Mexican provinces of Chihuahua and Sonora. The Ostend Manifesto was written in Buchanan's hand, and he never tired of saying, "We must have Cuba."

And yet men die, and die never to return; and all forms of social order draw us nearer to death, in so much as they take something away from us and give back nothing in exchange.
—Claude Lévi-Strauss, *Tristes Tropiques*

In Act II, my protagonist reads from a number of Buchanan's historical speeches. These are, in order:

"The kind Providence . . . throughout the world" and "Most happy . . . nearly forgotten": his Inaugural Address, given at Washington on March 4, 1857 [Moore, *Works*, Vol. X, pp. 105–113].

"We are indeed a nation . . . throughout the world": an address at a festival celebrating the establishment of a steamship line between Philadelphia and Liverpool, given at Philadelphia on January 11, 1851 [*Works*, Vol. VIII, pp. 405–411].

"What would I . . . admit everything" and "There are in our midst . . . every storm of faction": a speech to a Breckinridge rally from the portico of the White House, given on July 9, 1860 [*Works*, Vol. X, pp. 457–464].

"In order to justify . . . the last fatal plunge": his Fourth Annual Message to the Congress, given at Washington on December 3, 1860 [*Works*, Vol. XI, pp. 7–43].

"Mr. Mayor . . . in the country!": a speech given upon his return to Lancaster, March 6, 1861 [*Works*, Vol. XI, pp. 161–162].

In Act I, Anne Coleman quotes from, and George Coleman refers to, young Buchanan's oration of July 4, 1815, delivered before the Washington Association of Lancaster. The speech is wonderfully split in the *Works*, its first half appearing in Volume XII, pp. 316–320, and its second half in Volume I, pp. 2–9.

Many of the topical items with which Harriet entertains her uncle at the outset of Act III were adapted from the *Album of American History*, third volume (1853–1893), James Truslow Adams, editor-in-chief (1946).

And lest my middle-state characters' views of New England and its abolitionists seem fantastic, here is a paragraph from a letter written by Judge George W. Woodward, a politically active Philadelphian, to Attorney-General Black on November 18, 1860:

> Lloyd Garrison, offended with some trifle in the Colonization Society about 1835, & instigated not only by the D——l but by some English infidels, started the scheme of abolishing the Slavery of the U.S. He drew to himself all those Boston infidels whom unitarianism had thrown up to the surface & they commenced the war on Slavery. Their weapons were sometimes gross blasphemies—sometimes literary platitudes—sometimes humanitarian philosophies—but whichever they were, they were directed against Slavery, not because they cared for blacks or whites, but because Slavery was an Institution of civilized and Christianized Society. They saw the plain evidence that the principle of human bondage had received Divine sanction. This intensified their hate of it. They knew that we as a people were not responsible for the institution, but that we had dealt wisely with it and had turned it to good account—making it the instrument of blessing to both ourselves & the Slaves. This maddened their rage. Here was a chance to war against God, Native Country, political & social Institutions—and the vultures whetted their beaks for an unusual feast.

Judge Black, his reply stated, read this letter aloud "to the President and all the members of the Cabinet together. It excited universal admiration and approbation for its eloquence & its truth." [Auchampaugh, *JB and His Cabinet*, pp. 103, 109]

## Buchanan and Poetry

Poetry was a common thread in Buchanan's life, as in that of most Victorians. Apart from the poem to Anna Payne partially recited (the full three stanzas are given in Klein, p. 156), he is supposed to have written an earlier rhyming abdication to one Letitia Duncan:

> Her lovely hair in ringlets wave,
> And, hanging over her shoulder,
> She was fit to enter the heart
> Of any man who'd behold her.
> Her teeth were white, as the ivory showed,
> And her breath was spice, wherever it flowed,
> Her father was cruel,
> A sight of me he could not endure;
> The reason why? Because I was poor
> I dare not enter the dwelling
> Where dwells my lovely jewel.

The newspaper article containing this effusion has an air of the fabulous; but the obituary for Anne Coleman certainly contains three quoted lines:

> The spider's most attenuated thread
> Is cord, is cable, to man's tender tie
> On earthly bliss—it breaks at every breeze.

In his autobiographical sketch, Buchanan writes of his mother, "She had a great fondness for poetry, and could repeat with ease all the passages in her favorite authors which struck her fancy. These were Milton, Pope, Young, Cowper, and Thomson." Annie Buchanan, daughter of Edward, spent much time at Wheatland after her uncle's retirement; her long letter of reminiscence to Curtis contains the sentences, "My uncle was an extensive reader and had a good memory for what he had read. His reading embraced all classes of literature, and he conversed intelligently on all subjects." But his letters, compared with those of a florid Shakespeare- and Bible-monger like Jeremiah Black, do not show much ornament of quotation. In the most important speech of his life, his Fourth Annual Message to Congress on December 3, 1860, Buchanan did rise to Shakespearean echo, but then muddled it with rote phrases: "[The government] was not intended by its framers to be the baseless fabric of a vision, which, at the touch of the enchanter, would vanish into thin air, but a substantial and mighty fabric, capable of resisting the slow decay of time, and of defying the storms of ages."

Buchanan was the subject of poetry also. A Republican ditty went:

Who ever heard in all his life,
Of a candidate without a wife?

To another tune, Republicans sang:

As Buchanan was walking by the White House one day,
His eyes did roll upward, and thus he did say—
I am looking for lodgings, and this is the thing;
So I guess I will take it quite early next spring.

Published in Lancaster in 1856, *The Life of the Hon. James Buchanan as written by Himself and Set to Music by an Old Democrat*, in twelve stanzas of lame verse (leaning heavily on such meter-padding words as "then," "did," and "now," and showing the curious overuse of quotation marks characteristic of

semi-literacy) rehearses all of Buchanan's political sins up to
1856. His opportune shift from the Federalists to the Jackson
Democrats takes up the first seven, of which the last two run:

> The Feds of this country, they were an honest band;
> They first gave me office and honor in the land;
> They fed me like a "Buck"—I grew cunning as a "rat,"
> And I sniggered in my sleeve when I flogg'd a Democrat,
>> For a Federal pet was I.

> But things took a change, the Federal party fell,
> The whys and the wherefores I now dislike to tell,
> But Jackson's name and fame—they sav'd me from the
>> storm;
> I shouted for the man, but his honesty did scorn,
>> For a "wool-dyed" Fed was I.

The next stanza alludes to the notorious "Bargain and Sale"
controversy, that is, the accusation that Henry Clay, in the
no-decision election of 1824, threw his electoral votes to
Adams, enabling Adams to be elected President by the House
and receiving the Secretaryship of State in return. Buchanan,
then a young Congressman, was supposed (in the conversation reconstructed from varying accounts in my Act II) to
have made, on Clay's behalf, a similar proposition to Jackson,
who indignantly declined it.

> I labor'd with Jackson—his battles bravely fought—
> Of "Bargain and Sale" in thunder-tones did talk:
> I thundered down on Clay, as history does you tell;
> His honor I broke down, and Kentucky's hero fell,
>> For a Jackson Fed was I.

The last stanzas deal with Buchanan's fence-straddling and artful relativity:

> I've spoke against the Tariffs, I've voted for the same—
> 'Gainst banks I have thundered, and won a "ten cent"
>     fame,[18]
> I've had to fool the Dutch—the Yankees tickle nice,
> And with the "Nigger South" I've had to make a splice
>               For a candidate am I.
>
> I go for the South, the North, the East, the West,
> And for enslaving Kansas—I know it's for the best;
> The South "demands more room"—the West and North
>     must bow,
> And the East must knuckle down—and the Niggers hold
>     the plow,
>               For "Platform" James am I.
>
> I speak for the nation, I am the "Wheatland Sage,"
> And if not elected, the South will "bust with rage,"
> The "Union she'll dissolve," no "insults will she take,"
> Like electing Jack Fremont, for "selfish Freedom's" sake.
>               Well done—amen!—say I.
>
> I now close my life—the election's close at hand—
> Fremont you must defeat, with his "Free Kansas band";

---

[18]Reviving an old canard whereby Buchanan, speaking in support of Van Buren's Independent Treasury Bill, supposedly gave as an argument for it the possibility that the wages of labor would be reduced to ten cents a day. In fact, he had said something like the opposite, outlining the depressed conditions that would prevail unless banks were reformed. Though, as he said in a later speech, "There is no Democrat in the United States who will believe that any Senator could have the wickedness as well as folly to advocate the passage of any measure, upon the principle that it would lessen the reward of honest labor," the nickname stuck.

If this you fail to do, then Kansas will be free,
And I a martyr fall to the South and Slavery—
    And poor "Old Buck" will die!

And I too, when still attempting to make a novel of Buchanan's living and dying, found it tempting to cast a chapter—concerning his one attempt to go West—in the form of a frontier ballad:

## A Ballad of Kentucky
*(How Young James Buchanan, Having Completed His Preceptorship to James Hopkins, Esquire, of Lancaster, Travelled to Kentucky with the Thought of Starting Up a Practice There)*

> The spring of 1812 blew in,
>     The winds were fresh and raw;
> Old Hopkins told his protegé,
>     "My lad, go practice law."
>         A likely lad without a plan,
>         Our hero Jimmie Búchanán.*
>
> The apple trees went white with bloom,
>     The fields went green with wheat;
> A western restlessness began
>     To tickle Jimmie's feet.
>         A western destiny began
>         To tickle Jimmie Búchanán.
>
> The West lay empty as the sky,
>     And Mississippi trade

---

*Pronounced in the frontier manner, first and third syllables emphasized.

Was riding high on paddleboats;
   Here futures could be made:
      A country great, a future grand
      In store for Jimmie Búchanán.

His father owned a tract of land
   Whose title was awry
Beyond the dark Ohio flood
   In fabled Kéntucký:
      A litigated tract of land
      To lure young Jimmie Búchanán.

His father wrote and told him, "No,
   I didn't sacrifice
Your presence in my store so you
   Could trot to Paradise.
      Don't bother with my piece of land,
      My hasty Jimmie Búchanán."

"I'm twenty-one," the boy replied,
   "And need a change of air.
I'll bust my seams if I must spend
   My life in Lancaster.
      I want to win your piece of land,"
      Said stoutly Jimmie Búchanán.

He bought a horse, he bought a pack,
   He set him on his way
Across the Susquehanna tide
   Through Pennsylvani-ay.
      The horse and he topped thirteen span,
      Our mounted Jimmie Búchanán.

He rode all day, he rode all night,
   He never touched the loam
Until the roofs of Mercersburg
   Assured him he was home.
      Dunwoodie's doors shot forth the clan
      To welcome Jimmie Búchanán.

A brother, Edward, had been born,
   A sister, Jane, engaged;
His father muttered war was nigh,
   His mother dear had aged.
      All clustered, baby, gal, and man,
      Around our Jimmie Búchanán.

"O tarry here," his mother wept.
   "Life beckons," said her son.
"'Tis foolishness," his father swore,
   But blessed him, with a frown.
      "Our nation's march must have a van,"
      Said headstrong Jimmie Búchanán.

He twitched his horse's snaffle rein
   And westward held her nose;
The forest darkened like a curse,
   The Alleghenies rose.
      Night hid no braver bucko than
      Our hero Jimmie Búchanán.

Monongahela's mighty swell,
   Virginia's northern prong,
Ohio's winding valley maze
   Did not affright him long.

The endless miles, the endless land
Beguiled young Jimmie Búchanán.

The harness creaked upon the horse
  Whose blooded nostrils sighed,
Whose hoofbeats lulled the lonely path
    Through wilderness so wide;
      Through wilderness that dwindled Man
      Continued Jimmie Búchanán.

In virgin branches overhead
  A bird began to sing,
A bird with human voice announced,
    *"Young Jimmie, you are king:*
      *The center of a mighty span*
      *Of Otherness, young Búchanán.*

*"God has a single burning eye,*
  *That Eye is square on you;*
*Have faith and persevere! Fear not!*
  *Unto your star, be true!"*
      Thus clear the bubbling birdsong ran
      To sleepy Jimmie Búchanán.

At night, no cabin lights in view,
  He pillowed 'neath a tree
And prayed the panthers all about,
    And bears, to let him be.
      He slept with stars and woke with dawn,
      Our rugged Jimmie Búchanán.

He saw the raftsman ply his pole,
  The trapper skin his kill,

The farmer wrestle up his stumps
  Outside of Owingsville:
    A world was making, catch-as-can,
    Acknowledged Jimmie Búchanán.

He saw the backs of black men heave
  Beneath their heavy lot
And shine like welted fish: strange beasts,
  Not human, yet not not.
    The fate of slaves by Heaven's plan
    Bewildered Jimmie Búchanán.

He came upon a natural cave;
  The drip of lime within
Had laid a torchlit palace up
  In layers fine as skin.
    The cave of time since time began
    Astounded Jimmie Búchanán.

He bathed beneath a waterfall,
  His body battered pink.
He spilled his seed upon the earth
  And watched it palely sink.
    He sinned the sin of old Onan,
    Our youngster Jimmie Búchanán.

He prayed to ease his solitude,
  And lo! a shooting star
Made answer, far beyond a crag,
  Made answer, but so far.
    He sweated when he prayed, this tan
    Athletic Jimmie Búchanán.

The days when he had dwelt with men
   Receded in his mind;
His bond with all created things
   Transcended humankind.
      He grew to love the savage plan
      Of Nature, Jimmie Búchanán.

Each twig, each pine upon the ridge,
   Each whisper, trickle, start
Of wild life from the underbrush
   Etched bliss upon his heart.
      He grew to love the tender plan
      Of Nature, Jimmie Búchanán.

The westward weeks betrayed their goal;
   He reached Elizabethtown,
A wooden island lost within
   The Dark and Bloody Ground.
      Wild-looking as an Indian
      In trotted Jimmie Búchanán.

He found the courthouse, asked the judge
   How long his case might be;
The Judge replied, "It's been in court
   Since eighteen-hundred three."
      A litigated piece of land
      Frustrated Jimmie Búchanán.

"Well, well," said Jimmie to himself,
   "No nut too tough to crack.
I'll muster twenty arguments
   And break the deadlock's back."

So vowed the likely lad from Lan,
Lancáster, Jimmie Búchanán.

"I'll chop these woodsmen into bits
    With logic any day."
But who stood on the courthouse steps?
    John Pope and Henry Clay.
        Why howdy, little fancy Dan,"
        They said to Jimmie Búchanán.

John Rowan and John Allen too
    Adorned the local bar;
Perhaps the lad from Lancaster
    Had chased a fading star.
        The frontier never had a ban
        On lawyers, Jimmie Búchanán.

These long attorneys had an eye
    As beady as a squirrel's,
And front teeth filed like barrel sights,
    And fists like chestnut burls.
        They sized him up, a softer man,
        Our hero Jimmie Búchanán.

"Well, well," said Jimmie to himself,
    "This is a giant race.
At least back home in Lancaster
    The people know my face."
        He tied his pack and home he ran,
        Our hero Jimmie Búchanán.

"In Lancaster the fees are fat,
   The land is tame and sweet;
I feel an eastern destiny
   A-tingling in my feet."
      He whipped his horse and home he ran,
      Our hero Jimmie Búchanán.

Our hero Jimmie Búchanán
   Ne'er ventured west again,
But made his way, a winding way,
   Among domestic men.
      O what a rare American,
      Our hero, Jimmie Búchanán.

### Buchanan's Birthday

April 23rd: an auspicious one, shared with William Shakespeare, Vladimir Nabokov, Shirley Temple, Max Planck, Viscount Allenby, the historian Froude, the painter Turner, the composer Prokofiev, and the detested Stephen Douglas.

### Aleksandra Fedorovna

She was the daughter of Frederick William III, King of Prussia, and in 1817 married the prince who became Nicholas I of Russia. Seven years younger than Buchanan, she died seven years before he did. I was able to discover little else about her. The article on her in *La Grande Encylopédie* in its entirety reads:

*D'une santé délicate elle dut souvent quitter la Russie pour aller vivre à l'étranger. Son souvenir est resté populaire chez les Russes.*

*Susan Keitt*

One difference between fiction and history is that in fiction a minor character has no more existence than the author gives him, whereas in reality a person minor from one perspective is major from others, and always "round" instead of "flat." There is infinitely much to discover, and artistic proportion is menaced by research. I met Susan Keitt (pronounced *kit*) on page 172 of Nevins' second volume of *The Emergence of Lincoln*, in a passage concerning social life in Buchanan's Washington:

> An ingenuous view of Washington is afforded by the letters of Susanna Keitt, bride of the South Carolina Representative, who saw everything through unspoiled eyes. . . . A touching note is struck in her cry to her brother in the midst of the speakership contest—one of her repeated expressions of real fear:
> "Oh, Alec, we are having frightful times here—war any moment, and no knowing who may fall. . . . [Competing political factions] are armed and determined to fight to the knife there on the floor of Congress. . . . Oh, Alec, I am so uneasy I can write no more."
> This sensitive girl, terrified by the violent talk, bored by the bigwigs and wistful for the quiet pleasures of plantation life, found the receptions, dinners, and balls exhausting. . . . Buchanan insisted on seeing Mrs. Keitt, for Slidell said she

was the handsomest woman resident in Washington, and after her visit he gave a dinner party for her . . .

So I found her, and used her. It was my mistake, as I say, to place her first meeting with Buchanan a year later than it actually occurred—in the "secession winter" instead of the winter of the House Speakership struggle. But the name "Susanna" (which I eagerly seized, as containing a shade of "Anne") seems to be Nevins' invention; her husband's letters salute her as "Susie," her mother's call her "Susan," and she signs herself spondaically "Sue Sparks Keitt."

The Keitt correspondence, at Duke University, is fascinating, as history and as the record of a great love; an edited publication of these letters would, if not surpass the correspondence of Héloïse and Abélard, provide an American variant—with the man, in this case, the more ardent. Nevins does not exaggerate Mrs. Keitt's initial timorousness in Washington: other sections of the letter to her brother Alex [sic] read: "I'm so uneasy and nervous it will be a relief to talk with you. . . . Bowie knives and revolvers are the companions of every southern member. These are fearful times, and gloom and the most painful suspense and expectation prevail over the city. Heaven help us all."

That Buchanan was quite taken with her is amply corroborated. Keitt himself wrote, on January 17, 1860, that "The President has taken a chivalric devotion to her. If you want anything the President can give, just tell her, for she can command anything." She consented to meeting him reluctantly: "Mr. Mann says the President is anxious to see me and wondered why I had not called and begged him to bring me around. I have no fancy for the story-telling old man, but as Mr. Keitt and Mr. Mann wish me to go, and Mr. Buchanan particularly requested it, I shall go around some evening this week." [December 4, 1859] In the event, he was more favorably impressed than she: "Then in came the old President. He has one of the most quizzical faces I ever saw—Head and mouth twisted to one side, and then the erratic performances of that *famous eye!* He made himself very agreeable and cordially pressed me to let him see me often." [December 22, 1859] The cordiality persisted through at least that winter: "The old President was extremely gracious; they say I am rather a favorite at the White House" [January 26, 1860]; "The old President begged me to come up and ride with Miss Lane, but the weather has been too bad all winter for gentlemen even to ride" [February 25, 1860].

Susan the person, however, diverges from Susanna the character in the rapid raising of her political consciousness. The nervous newcomer of late 1859, who earlier that year had been writing bitterly from Europe, "That I should so study and plan and dream of foreign lands, and it all to end in this: a little flying tour among the flat-headed Dutch and disgusting Swiss and then return home," by February of 1860 is parroting her husband's Dixie chauvinism:

> I am in favor of Douglas because southern men can rule him and get what they want—and then he is in favor of taking Cuba and all those other southern enterprises. The only way the South can save herself is to spread south, get new territory, enlarge herself, and spread her institutions, and cut loose from the North.

By the time of Lincoln's inaugural, Mrs. Keitt, in a long letter to a former Washington friend in Philadelphia, sounds like some Rebel Amazon:

> And if the fate of Carthagenia be ours, we women, like those of old, will cut our hair for bowstrings to plague the

enemy as long as possible. . . . You still hope for reunion. A vain hope unless our conditions be accepted. Here they are—Hang all your Redpaths, Garrisons, Greelys, and Ward Beechers, incarcerate your Gerrit Smiths, unite your Sumners and Sewards to ebony spouses and send them as *resident ministers in perpetuum* to Timbuctoo, purge the halls of Congress and the White House of the odor of their presence and attach the death penalty to all future agitators of the slavery question. [March 4, 1861]

Nor are her martial spirits dampened by war when it comes. In April of 1864, in a letter to Dudley Mann in Paris, she describes herself standing with Keitt overlooking Charleston harbor:

Oh my God, it was a scene to make one shout and weep. I stood upon the porch looking on, with my brave soldier beside me and my little ones sleeping peacefully in their bed. What though danger encompassed me and hurtled in the air, our lot was here cast and we must bravely bear it to the end. That it will be a triumphant end no one dares dispute. . . . Were it not for my children I would follow the drum. I must learn to be a good soldier, you know, for were our glorious army to be crushed, every woman of the South must take the field. I teach my children daily to hate the Yankees. . . . But the clouds of gloom so long hanging over us are now parting and we see in the brightening sky the Southern Cross gleaming in prophetic splendor.

Shortly afterwards, in the folder of letters, come the telegrams confusedly announcing her husband's wound, and then his death, at Charleston.

Keitt himself, in his letters to her, writes less pointedly, with a stupefying fluency of deluded rhetoric. The subject of the Confederacy makes him virtually delirious:

Man dies; the nation, never or seldom. It has its sleep, its long trance, its dreams, its night walking; but it does not die. In its deepest trance it is ready for the silver hour of the promised prince. It looks down into the dark gulf with firmness, and up to the golden height hopefully. The mirage wraps you round. The delusions are not as to existence; they are only as to place and time. Sail on and you will meet the very ship you saw in the air. Its figure was inverted, but it is now erect. [February 19, 1861]

He justifies slavery with exceptional serenity, though the pompous sociology was standard Southern doctrine:

I mean to show, also, that certain duties, necessary in the regimen of society, are antagonistic to mental culture and, therefore, that civilization is highest which rescues the improving and ruling race from their performance—alias the South through slavery. [June 19, 1856]

The affair of "Bully Brooks" brings out a streak of, more than brutality, jubilant recklessness:

Brooks that day flogged Sumner of Massachusetts, and did it well and soundly. He combined in happy proportion freedom of speech and freedom of the cudgel. . . . If the northern men had stood up, the city would now float with blood. . . . Everybody here feels as if we are upon a volcano. I am glad of it, for I am tired of stagnation. [May 29, 1856]

When the volcano explodes, he writes as if of toy soldiers:

> I want you, dear Susie, to see my regiment. The men are getting into their new uniforms and they are looking famous. You must see them before the gloss gets off. [January 21, 1862]

And as the war grinds on—the war that he and his fellow fire-eaters had invited, against the good sense and forebodings not only of wary Northerners like Buchanan but of the Southern commonality as well—Keitt, blind to his own guilt, clings amid the carnage to the most preposterous illusions:

> One thing I firmly believe, viz., that the institution of slavery is and will be unshaken, come what may . . . My own conviction is that anti-slavery is dying out . . . [January 22, 1864]

The North is not fighting fair: "War in any aspect is cruel, but this war is robbed of chivalry." [January 24, 1864] Earlier he had predicted that the war must soon end because prolonged war is "against the genius of civilization and the Christianity which underlies the conduct of modern nations." [May 4, 1862] The day before he received his fatal wound, he assured his wife that, though his own troops "feel as if led by the hand of Providence," "Grant brings his men up only by making them drunk." [May 31, 1864]

One can forgive Keitt much, however, for the great uxorious love he bore. At first, Susie had proved elusive, breaking one engagement and finally consenting to marriage in 1858 on the promise of a long tour of Europe, where she wanted to study art. In his courting letters, along with the racist, secessionist fustian runs the plaintive note of a man trying to sell himself.

Pleasantly, after I had him call her his "firefly" onstage, I came upon a punning sentence: "You have been a promethean spark and I have relumed a spirit which was slightly waning and given a brighter blaze to fires which were somewhat fitfully burning." [February 17, 1856][19] Once he captured her in marriage, his passion blazes even higher. He signs his letters, "Your lover-husband," and accepts his newly born daughter on the basis that she somewhat resembles his wife: "At first I did not think her pretty, but now that her features have become defined and the angles made clear and softened, she is beautiful. She has her mother's fingers and nose—in fact, many of her mother's features. If she turns out to be half as good as her Mama I shall be satisfied." [May 11, 1860][20] From battle he wrote his wife:

> I don't think I fear death more than a gentleman ought—I may say I know I don't—but I do hate to leave you. But for that, I think I should be pretty indifferent. . . . I would part with my little daughters and it would be a sore and terrible anguish, but to part from you cracks every chord of the spirit and soul. . . . I almost fear that you are my religion. [May 1, 1862]

The Reverend Dr. Pryor, who attended Keitt in his last agonies, "after some conversation on spiritual matters," heard him utter these final words: "Oh, wife. Wife." By another account, the invocation was triple: "Oh, wife. Wife. Wife."

---

[19]How labored, though, is this compared to her own little warm simile: "I can no more stand cold weather than can a tomato plant." [from Washington, January 26, 1860]

[20]A letter of hers states: "Mr. Keitt spoke truly when he told Mr. Brown he cared nothing for children. However, all the devotion he can spare from my fortunate self he gives to his little daughter." [January 1861] This was the first daughter, Anna, or "Annita" (1860–1919). The second daughter lived only four years (1861–1865). Her name is given variously as Ethel or Stella.

## Mary Ann Cobb and Kate Thompson

The wives of two Southern members of Buchanan's Cabinet, Howell Cobb and Jacob Thompson, corresponded whenever one of them—usually Mrs. Cobb—was out of Washington. Howell Cobb resigned from the Cabinet on December 8, 1860, and Thompson exactly one month later; but the Thompsons stayed on in Washington some more months, and Kate Thompson's letters to her friend in Georgia form a primary source for details during this critical winter—her long letter of January 13th, for example, tells us that Thompson went three nights without sleep in unravelling the Indian bonds theft, that Buchanan asked Breckinridge to invite Floyd to resign, that Floyd refused, that Thompson not only felt betrayed by the sailing of the *Star of the West* but doubted that Buchanan himself knew about it, that Washington gossip reported that Forney wanted to make up with the President, that the city appeared deserted and the government departments were all filled with guns. She was, Kate Thompson, a remarkable woman (she might have dominated my play, had I let her in)—married at fourteen, as a poor, uneducated Mississippi girl, to the *arriviste* lawyer and landowner, who without consummating the marriage sent her off to Paris for four years of schooling. In her early thirties, as the most vivacious and attractive of the Cabinet wives, she was a pet of the President, occupying for a time that hungry, empty place in Buchanan's heart that Susan Keitt at a later moment was pushed into. Her letters, on their little neat rectangles of notepaper, greet the researcher as oases of legibility and pert observation in the scribbled expanses of the voluminous Cobb papers at the University of Georgia; they are strikingly free of that fluff, pious and familial, so abundant in the letters of Southern women such as Leonora Clayton and Mary Ann Cobb. Though their general documentary value has been long appreciated, and their details have passed into the texture of the era's history—Nevins, Nichols, and Klein all draw on them, not always with acknowledgment— I travelled to Athens to consult Kate Thompson's letters afresh, in the hope of finding some intimate glimmer cast upon the President personally.

Buchanan fascinated her, in a disagreeable way; one feels he made her flesh crawl.

> I went with the President & Miss Lane to the *Oritorio*, at Dr. Hall's Church—such a stupid, tiresome time I had— I could hardly keep my eyes open—and it lasted 'till 10 o'clock, but just *think*, the President staid 10 minutes and made his escape at a side door. I felt truly happy, when I looked around & saw he was gone. [May 1, 1859]

The P.S. to this same early letter reads:

> This letter is so full of gossip & small talk, I venture to say the *President, himself* would enjoy reading it.

She implies something unhealthy, too, in Buchanan's close attentions to Howell Cobb, during his wife's absence:

> ... but he [Cobb] does not come to take a meal with us, half as often as I wish, for the President has taken complete possession of him since you left and he drives there nearly every day & when he is missing, the President calls upon him, to give an account of himself, so you see, he has gained no additional freedom by your going home. [May 18, 1859]

An unexpectedly corporeal glimpse of Buchanan is afforded further on, when Kate tells him that Harriet's New York escort, Martin Van Buren's son, is known as Prince John Van Buren—"when I told the Chief about this, he shook his fat sides laughing." When Harriet stays away, Kate complains:

> I wish she would come back. The old *Chief* takes particular pleasure in saying, "I do not care how long she stays. I can do very well without her"—which always makes me feel a little mad at him—but who can expect any thing better from such a *hardened* old Bachelor—however, he had a good time in N. Carolina, for Mr. T. says he kissed hundreds of pretty girls—which made his *mouth water.* [June 8, 1859]

This game, of teasing the old President's libido, seems widespread at least among the Southern half of the Cabinet. Later that summer, Howell Cobb writes Mary Ann,

> The President Miss Lane Mrs. Thompson & Macon—and Mrs. Bass left on Monday for Bedford. The old gentleman seemed in excellent spirits at the idea of having so many ladies in his party. He was especially tickled at the presence of Mrs. Bass who is making serious inroads upon his affections. The absence of Mrs. Craig—and her reported engagement with Mr. Robb—has induced the President to look about for a new lover on whom to bestow his smiles of love . . . [July 20, 1859]

Kate, meanwhile, has written a comic description of Buchanan's dressing himself up for Mrs. Bass and dismisses some gossip hinting at an improper alliance between herself and

her correspondent's husband—one wonders how compla-
cently this tidbit was received back at Cobbham. A summer
later, rather puzzlingly, Kate refers to Buchanan's *"overpower-
ing"* reaction to Mrs. Cobb's long absence—"I have a great
[deal] to say on this subject which I must keep until I see you."
[August 7, 1860]

Mrs. Cobb returns to Washington, and when the curtain
goes up on the correspondence again, Cobb has resigned, and
the storm has lowered. On December 15, 1860, Kate writes:

> I go to see her [Harriet Lane] & the President as often as I
> can because I know they feel their old friends are many of
> them deserting them—I will do all I can to stand by them
> until the 4th of March—& hope that day may come
> quickly ... Dr. Maynard (the gun man) has been here two
> hours trying to sell Mr. Thompson 3,000 Guns—so my
> head is nearly crazy & my heart goes *pit a pat* at any sound
> I hear. What are we all coming to?

A month goes by, and we come to betrayal, resignation, and
fury. From the well-known letter of January 13/14:

> ... Gov. Floyd resigned Saturday morning—the President
> behaved as mean[21] as he could about this matter ... Tues-
> day morning (Jan 8) Mr. T. sent his resignation to the

---

[21]"Mean" seems a weak word to express outrage, but her husband uses it also,
writing Cobb on January 16th about these same events: "The President and Holt
played the meanest trick on me in the world in sending the Star of the West to
Charleston ... Old Buck, at heart, is right & with us. But after Stanton came in, I
have seen him gradually giving way. He is so infirm in purpose that I do not know
what to expect of him. Neither Black, Holt or Stanton have any commonsense, and
hence all the President's difficulties—& he has had the horrors for fear of
impeachment—and the withdrawal of Senators on account of the secession of our
States."

President—and his answer accepting it, I think the most infamous letter ever written by any man—After all Mr. T. had done in trying to sustain him—to receive such treatment. I was boiling hot—but Mr. T. resented it in a very decided, but mild answer—which drew a very affectionate answer from the President—but this did not satisfy me.[22] I hate the old man worse than ever . . . I do not believe there is an honest man in Pennsylvania. . . .[23] The last week that Mr. T. was in the cabinet Judge B., Holt and Stanton gave him unmistakable evidences of their desire for him to leave—but Mr. T. still insisted the President's *heart* was with us and he would never send the troops. Now you can guess what I think of the President's heart.

What she thinks, perhaps, is what she always thought—there was something queer about it, that made her uncomfortable. Later in this long letter, she describes Buchanan's social position:

My dear Mrs. Cobb, the President has not a friend in the world . . . *all their* old friends are thrown off and new ones in their places. I feel as light and happy as a *bird I am out, yes out of the Union* too.

This last sentence recalls not only Lawrence Keitt's cry that he feels like a boy let out from school but her own strange relief, in church two springs ago, at looking around and finding the President gone.

---

[22]These four letters were preserved, and can be found in Moore, *Works*, Vol. XI, pp. 100–1, 102–3, and 104.

[23]Like Henry Adams, in his letters of some weeks previously (see epigraphs), she has been brought to the conclusion that "Pennsylvania is rotten to the core."

And still Kate is not done with him. Amazingly, Buchanan invited the Thompsons to a farewell dinner at the White House; and they went. "I went in with the Old Chief. Mr. T. with Miss Lane—& Genl. Dix (who is staying there) with Mrs. Ellis. . . . There was nothing disagreeable said or done, but I felt very much embarrassed. The President asked me at dinner who was to be *our President*." [February 3, 1861][24] Even back in Mississippi, she ponders the clinging muddle of her feelings about Buchanan: ". . . for I nearly hate *the old chief* and if he was not such an old man I would—besides there are many reasons why I should like him and I intend to try to do as near right as I can." [April 17, 1861]

In Kate Thompson's letters we draw close enough to Buchanan to shudder. He is uncanny, unnatural. Though Kate does not, as did Susan Keitt, express repugnance for his quizzical face and erratic eye, she registers, as if thermally, a clammy chill, confusingly mixed with his fat, stiff teasability and oppressive show of affection. Outrageously, this impotent "old chief" in crisis develops, or borrows from his fellow-Pennsylvanians Stanton and Black, the power to deny, to cast out the South, though his "*heart* was with us." In her sex, Kate has always felt uneasy with Buchanan. "I hate the old man worse than ever"—to how far back does that "ever" extend? Her letters show a pattern of fascination (in even the briefest of her notes, she mentions "The President"), condescension ("our great self-made man" [June 10, 1859]), and unease bordering on revulsion and hatred; in this pattern Anne Coleman's ghost is moving, somehow, taking its revenge.

---

[24]Quoted by Klein, p. 401. The original, regrettably, is now missing from the Cobb papers in Athens.

*Glimpses of Buchanan*

When the Cincinnati convention nominated Buchanan in 1856, Murat Halstead wrote, "The selection of Mr. Buchanan is in itself an equivocation—his only quality being the absence of all qualities . . . what idea to the people of this Union does the name of James Buchanan suggest? None."[25] And it is true, glimpses of this long-public man that bring us within sniffing distance of his skin are rare. An 1854 book of verbal caricatures, George W. Bungay's *Off-Hand Takings; or, Crayon Sketches of the Noticeable Men of our Age*, contains Webster, Clay, Frémont, Edward Everett, even Pierre Soulé, but *not* Buchanan. Jeremiah Black's biographer W. N. Brigance wrote of Buchanan, "Of all men in modern history, none is harder with whom to make acquaintance."[26] A virulent anti-Federalist broadside of July 1820, signed "Colebrook" in allusion to the Coleman tragedy of the winter before (if not actually signifying authorship by one of the Coleman brothers), begins, "To James Buchanan, Esquire—Allow me to congratulate you upon the notoriety you have acquired of late. Formerly the smoothness of your looks and your habitual professions of moderation had led those who did not know you to suppose you mild & temperate." The letter goes on to accuse the young political aspirant of "virulence" in accusing Governor Findlay of owning a Negro slave. Buchanan won election to the House of Representatives, however, and his long national career commenced. In 1832, Anne Royall, the

---

[25] Halstead feels this strongly, and says the same thing many times: "He stands nowhere. He never did stand anywhere. . . . this experienced and veteran camp-follower has learned, if nothing else, the benefits of non-committalism, and the art of holding his dish right side up, whatever may be the direction of the shower. . . ."

[26] Brigance, *Black*, p. 71.

first of America's gushing female journalists, wrote in the
third volume of her *Black Book* (p. 134), "Hon. *J. Buchanan* of
Pa. is almost a giant in size, as well as mind. No description
that the most talented writer could give, can convey an idea of
Mr. Buchanan; he is quite a young man (and a batchelor, ladies) with a stout handsome person; his face is large and fair,
his eye, a soft blue, one of which he often shuts, and has a
habit of turning his head to one side . . ." *La soleil ni la mort ne
se peuvent regarder fixement.*

President Polk, his gaze sharpened by his conviction that
Buchanan was maneuvering to succeed him, recorded a number of glimpses, and in one diary entry (September 1, 1846)
conceded, as few contemporaries did, greatness to the man:
"Mr. B. is a man of talents & is fully competent to discharge
the high duties of Secy of State, but it is one of his weaknesses
(and perhaps all great men have such) that he takes on &
magnifies small matters into great & undeserved importance." Nathaniel Hawthorne served as Liverpool consul
under Buchanan's ambassadorship to England, and his *English
Note-books* (January 6, 1855, a few days before he enjoyed
Harriet Lane's "firm-textured" conversation) describes Buchanan affably, even to the old man's blush. Also, however,
Hawthorne seems nervously alert for signs of deviousness.

> I like Mr. [Buchanan]. He cannot exactly be called gentle-
> manly in his manners, there being a sort of rusticity about
> him; moreover, he has a habit of squinting one eye, and an
> awkward carriage of his head; but, withal, a dignity in his
> large person, and a consciousness of high position and im-
> portance, which gives him ease and freedom. Very simple
> and frank in his address, he may be as crafty as other diplo-
> matists are said to be; but I see only good sense and plain-

ness of speech,—appreciative, too, and genial enough to make himself conversable. He talked very freely of himself and of other public people, and of American and English affairs. He returns to America, he says, next October, and then retires forever from public life, being sixty-four years of age, and having now no desire except to write memoirs of his times, and especially of the administration of Mr. Polk. I suggested a doubt whether the people would permit him to retire; and he immediately responded to my hint as regards his prospects for the Presidency. He said that his mind was fully made up, and that he would never be a candidate, and that he had expressed this decision to his friends in such a way as to put it out of his own power to change it. He acknowledged that he should have been glad of the nomination for the Presidency in 1852, but that it was now too late, and that he was too old,—and, in short, he seemed to be quite sincere in his *nolo episcopari;* although, really, he is the only Democrat, at this moment, whom it would not be absurd to talk of for the office. As he talked, his face flushed, and he seemed to feel inwardly excited. Doubtless, it was the high vision of half his lifetime which he here relinquished. I cannot question that he is sincere; but, of course, should the people insist upon having him for President, he is too good a patriot to refuse. I wonder whether he can have had any object in saying all this to me. He might see that it would be perfectly natural for me to tell it to General Pierce [Hawthorne's close friend]. But it is a very vulgar idea,—this of seeing craft and subtlety, when there is a plain and honest aspect.

A more worldly observer, the Russian revolutionary and memoirist Alexander Herzen, also met Buchanan in his London years, and with a witty "therefore" reconciles craft and aspect: "The sly old man Buchanan, who was then already dreaming, in spite of his seventy years, of the presidency, and therefore was constantly talking of the happiness of retirement, of the idyllic life and of his own infirmity . . ." Buchanan at this time was not seventy but a few months short of sixty-three. The occasion was the somewhat notorious diplomatic dinner given by the United States consul in London, George Sanders, for an assortment of European radicals in exile. Herzen, though he attended (along with Mazzini, Kossuth, Ledru-Rollin, and Garibaldi), viewed the affair as one of President Pierce's "schoolboy pranks" intended to divert liberal Europe from "the main jewel on which his whole policy turned—the imperceptible expansion and consolidation of slavery." (The truth was more Machiavellian still: the overthrow of the monarchies of the Old World held out to the imperialists of the New the hope of annexing Cuba.) Herzen, according to his *My Past and Thoughts*, rather sourly watched Buchanan bestow compliments all around with a manner "much more reminiscent of an experienced diplomatist than of the austere citizen of a democratic republic," and, when his conversational term came, received in silence Buchanan's genial statement that he had brought away from his time in Russia "the conviction that she had a great future." Then, however, Herzen recalled a twenty-year-old, very lonely glimpse of Buchanan at the tsar Nicholas's coronation: "I was a boy, but you were so conspicuous in your simple, black frock-coat and round hat, in that crowd of embroidered, gilded, uniformed notables." The very day of this dinner with revolutionaries, Buchanan had written to Harriet, "Tomorrow will be the first levee of the Queen, & my appearance there in a suit of plain clothes will, I have no doubt, produce quite a sensation & become a subject of gossip for the whole court." As it turned out, his costume, a black suit augmented by a black-hilted dress sword to distinguish him from the servants, did nicely; he wrote Harriet afterwards, "The dress question, after much difficulty, has been finally & satisfactorily settled. . . . I must confess that I never felt more proud of being an American, than when I stood in that brilliant circle, 'in the simple dress of an American citizen.' " A spot of black in a sea of gilt.

Once Buchanan occupied the White House, there was no lack of vivid portraits:

Up to his elbows in papers and up to his neck in political mischief—sits the Old Public Functionary! He is arrayed in a long dressing-gown and slippers, holds an unlighted cigar in his mouth and has a peculiar nervous twitching always to the left as if some unseen spirits were plucking him on that side by the sleeve and whispering distasteful counsel . . .

Mr. B. has a shrill, almost female voice, and wholly beardless cheeks; and he is not by any means, in any aspect the sort of man likely to cut, or attempt to cut his throat for any Chloe or Phillis in Pennsylvania.

Auchampaugh, who quotes both these libels from Douglas papers of 1860, argues against the first that many men wore dressing gowns, including President Pierce; and against the second that Buchanan grew a pair of muttonchop whiskers while in England, and there are portraits to prove it. The Chicago *Tribune*, on January 3, 1861, reported that "The old man has become little better than a sot. He keeps saturated with Monongahela whiskey. He drinks to drown remorse and stupefy his brain as he staggers along with the treasonable gang who have possession of him."

One of the treasonable gang, William Henry Trescot, a brilliant diplomatist from South Carolina who acted as an intermediary for the South Carolina "Commissioners" and who had earlier served under Buchanan in the London mission, wrote in 1861 a "Narrative" concerning the eventful negotiations of December 1860. His characterization of the President, though unkind, is keen, and historians have drawn especially upon this one long sentence:

> Cold and calculating, with a clear head but no heart, ready at any moment to desert a friend whom he had used in order to secure an enemy whom he wanted to use—with a habit of indirectness that at times almost became falsehood and a wariness that sometimes degenerated into craftiness—with no faith in sentiment and a cynical estimate of men the result of long party experience, and all this justified in his own eyes by the fact, which nobody can dispute who knows him, that he really had no ulterior selfish purpose—that he wished to serve his country and was a man in his individual relations of perfectly clean hands—Mr Buchanan was just the man to utterly belittle a great cause, misunderstand a real national crisis and compromise a great position by small acts and smaller motives.

Perhaps the most thoughtful impression of Buchanan occurs in *Casket of Reminiscences* (1874), by the Unionist Senator from Mississippi, Henry S. Foote.

> I knew James Buchanan for many years, and intimately. . . . I had every opportunity, alike in private life and

amid the turmoil and excitement of political controversy, to learn his real temper and character, so as now to be able to speak of them with something approaching to authority. He was undoubtedly a man of solid and vigorous intellect, without having the least claim, though, to be ranked as a man of genius. . . . His knowledge of the ancient classic writers was exceedingly imperfect, and he was far from being at all familiar with any of the renowned British authors who, in prose and verse, have filled up the space of years between Chaucer and Macaulay. When a member of the Senate of the United States, though his intellectual powers must have been then in their prime, he was not known to deliver a single speech remarkable either for eloquence, for potential reasoning, or for valuable practical illustration. He was notably deficient both in ingenuity and in rhetorical brilliancy. I do not think he ever uttered a genuine witticism in his life; though, on social occasions, he was often more or less facetious, and, in what Dryden calls "the horseplay of raillery," was indeed quite an adept. Nobody, though, ever heard him talk stupidly or ignorantly; and whenever a subject chanced to be introduced with which he felt himself to be unacquainted he had the good sense to be obdurately and unmovedly silent. . . .[27]

---

[27] Against this surprisingly caustic sketch by his old crony should be set James Buchanan Henry's assertion that "Mr. Buchanan had an extraordinary memory, and could repeat verbatim much of the classic authors of his college days" [*Works*, XII, p. 319]; Klein's statement that, in the inactive years of 1849–1852, when Buchanan, retired from the Department of State and not yet assigned the London mission, lived in his new home of Wheatland the life of a country squire, he read not only such historical works as Jared Sparks' *Life of Washington* and Madison's newly published notes on the Constitutional Convention but "a good many of Sir Walter Scott's novels and the writings of Charles Dickens" [p. 210]; and Annie Buchanan's remembrance that besides his daily recourse to the Bible and Jay's *Exercises* her uncle "read a great deal in the sermons of the great French

That he was himself a man of inflexible integrity I do not think admits of question; though it is yet not altogether forgotten, and perhaps never will be, that in the earlier part

---

preacher, Massillon, a French copy of which he had and often quoted." [Curtis, II, p. 678]

Annie recalls his conversation with delight: "My uncle had the most delightful way of throwing himself back into the past scenes of his life, and, as it were, living them over again. He would tell you the whole position of affairs, make you understand the point of the story thoroughly, and then laugh in a most infectious way." [Curtis, II, p. 675]

Nor are Buchanan's letters devoid of humorousness. Writing to Mr. Johnston, Harriet's husband, on November 14, 1867, declining an invitation to Baltimore with the explanation that "the idea of becoming dangerously ill away from home deters me from going abroad," Buchanan describes a fall: "On Saturday last, supposing that I was at the head of the steps on the front porch, I took a step forward as if on the level, and fell with my whole weight on the floor, striking my head against one of the posts. Thanks to the thickness and strength of my skull, it was not broken, and the only bad consequence from it is a very black eye."

And writing flirtatiously to a Miss Emily Baker on the first day of the year of his death: "I think I can see you standing gracefully on the highest pinnacle of Ritualism and taking your flight over to Romanism. You will not have a difficult passage to the dome of St. Peter's."

In a compendium of "The Wit of the Presidents," I found Buchanan represented by one witticism, given as, "We have met the enemy and we are theirs." This is from his letter to Harriet on October 15, 1858; the night before, the disastrous consequences of his Lecompton stand had registered in an emphatic anti-Buchanan sweep of Pennsylvania. Nevins, in his *Emergence* (Vol. I, p. 400), appears primly offended by this letter: "Seldom if ever has a President taken so sharp a discomfiture with such levity."

What Buchanan had written was, "Well! We have met the enemy in Pennsylvania & we are theirs." Further on, this paragraph:

"Judge Black, General Anderson of Tennessee, Mr. Brenner, & Mr. Van Dyke dined with me yesterday, & we had a merry time of it, laughing among other things over our crushing defeat. It is so great that it is almost absurd."

Such a mood in the old gentleman, probably less unusual than we imagine, takes us back to the days at Dickinson, when he danced on table tops in the tavern backrooms and, one Fourth of July, downed sixteen regular toasts before starting on the volunteers. [Klein, p. 9]

Finally, in this unconscionably farraginous footnote to the moot matter of glimpses, should be included the eulogy volunteered by Buchanan's black barber in Lancaster: "Why, sir, he didn't know what it was to give a rough answer to man, woman, or child." Which accords with Mary Sherry's, "I liked him so, he was so good."

of his political career he had been known once or twice to have become involved in perplexing predicaments which exposed him to the suspicion of being a little insincere and ambidextrous in matters of political management. . . .

Mr. Buchanan had always professed to hold in great horror the doctrines of the extreme State's rights school of the South. . . . But he had, in some way, learned to dread the fierce audacity of the Southern fire-eaters, as he was accustomed to call them, and it several times became obvious to me, long before he fell under their domination in 1860, that his fear of the leaders of this blustrous and menacing faction was not wholly unmixed with something of a respectful admiration.

Which last suggestion is more interesting than Foote himself admits; I tried to use it. Of two curious glimpses I may have overused, one, the tale that Buchanan as a young child wore a bell about his neck so he could wander freely in the forest around Stony Batter, appears in *Recollections of College Life at Marshall College, Mercersburg, Pa., from 1839–1845*, by the Reverend Theodore Appel (Reading, Pa., 1886), in a passage too piquant not to quote:

Little "Jamie," with his bright blue eyes and his fair white skin, was as happy as the little brook that flowed smiling along below the house. His mother, engaged in household duties, or assisting the father in attending to the customers in the store, according to tradition, was accustomed to put a cow-bell around his neck in the morning, so that she could always hear where he was during the day, or find him if he wandered too far away and lose himself among the thickets. This was a wise precaution, because the mountains were still infested with bears, wild-cats and panthers, and it was dangerous for grown persons to venture out too far without a gun.

The other glimpse, the story that Buchanan expressed the wish to return reincarnated as a frog in his own spring, occurs (among other places) in Philip Shriver Klein's small book *The Story of Wheatland*. The spring figures also in the reminiscences of Mary Sherry, who, when interviewed in 1929 in the Lancaster almshouse by Ida L. K. Hofstetter for her article "Harriet Lane," recalled,

> I liked him so, he was so good. . . . I was with him when he died and when I brought some of the cold water from the spring for him at night he said,—"Oh! Mary, that is too much for you; you have worked all night and are tired and it is lonely and dark down there" (referring to the spring on his own ground and of which water he was very partial) and then she [responded] "I will bring you water from the spring as long as you can drink it."

Mary Sherry, then in her mid-nineties, must have been the last living person to have known and touched Buchanan.

## Apologia Pro Opere Suo

The Kierkegaard quote, about the man with two differing eyes, to whom everything was very relative, excited me nearly twenty years ago; I, too, "wanted to write a novel in which the chief character" etc. To this fallow inspiration (I did try a few dozen pages, the journal of a wicked man, a high school principal) time added the idea of a novel with a stationary hero, a man in bed dying. Learning that Samuel Beckett, Hermann Broch, and Carlos Fuentes had already written such books dampened but not quite extinguished this ambition, which was vaguely intermixed with a youthful vision of a tetralogy, of which the first novel would be set in the future, the second in the present, the third in the remembered past, and the fourth in the historical past. The first three materialized obediently enough (*The Poorhouse Fair*, *Rabbit, Run*, and *The Centaur*), but the fourth hung unachieved, attracting to itself, over the years, the lint and interstellar matter of fragmentary inspirations. The discovery that Buchanan had mismatched eyes fitted the Kierkegaard, and the fact that he was Dying worked in with an over-all alphabetical scheme of writing in my lifetime twenty-six novels, each to be dominated by one letter of the alphabet—the "B" in *Rabbit, Run* and the "C" in *The Centaur* need scarcely be emphasized. But while I waited for the "D" to pull together (the first sentence would go, *During the night, the old man had a strange dream*), many other books presented themselves to be mustered through the presses, and the tetralogy remained open on one side to the wind and bad weather.

James Buchanan had to be the historical figure. Who was he? In my Pennsylvania childhood, I knew him to be the only President our great and ancient state had produced; but where were the monuments, the Buchanan Avenues, the extollatory juvenile volumes with titles like *Jimmie Buchanan, Keystone Son in the White House* or *"Old Buck," the Hair-Splitter Who Preceded the Rail-Splitter?* Lincoln and Washington were drummed into us but Buchanan went unmentioned. When, in 1968, as an act of penance for a commercially successful novel set in New England, I began my research, I discovered,

AFTERWORD

of course, that Buchanan's administration had ended under a cloud of disgrace that after a century still glowered. The Covode Investigation, the Floyd scandals, General Scott's published charges, a campaign of press vilification led by Forney, Greeley, and Bennett, the Lincoln administration's self-serving innuendoes,[28] a congressional vendetta that stooped to abolishment of the franking privilege of ex-Presidents and to Thaddeus Stevens's claim that Buchanan had defrauded the government of eight thousand dollars for White House furnishings—all did their work. Not Buchanan's tediously dispassionate self-defense, nor the grand and tragic fatalism which informs Lincoln's second inaugural—giving the war the cast of divine foreordination, of an inexorable justice whereby "every drop of blood drawn with the lash, shall be paid by another drawn with the sword"—could dissipate the impression of bad performance and worse faith on Buchanan's part. Even modern historians, a century remote from the wounds of the Civil War, sometimes jeer vindictively at "Poor, foolish Buchanan!" who "prayed and twittered and did nothing." [Samuel Eliot Morison, *The Oxford History of the American People* (1965), pp. 593, 608]

And yet my grandfather John Hoyer, born in Berks County in 1863, spoke of Lincoln as of someone who had personally swindled him, and to his death at the age of ninety voted the straight Democratic ticket. I felt a mystery here. My father,

---

[28]Lincoln, in his war message of July 4, 1861, found that "A disproportionate share of the federal muskets and rifles had somehow found their way into these [seceding] states, and had been seized," that "The Navy was scattered in distant seas," and that his efforts to reinforce Fort Pickens were frustrated by "some *quasi* armistice of the late administration." In the next paragraph, however, he cashes in resoundingly the net result of the unmartial Buchanan policy: "It is thus seen that the assault upon, and reduction of, Fort Sumter, was in no sense a matter of self-defence on the part of the assailants."

born Republican, became a Roosevelt Democrat in the Depression; this was understandable, the Depression was in my
marrow. (And the opprobrium that attached to Hoover in the
1930's, if heightened by imputations of treason and the fact of
a million wartime casualties, approximates Buchanan's disgrace.) John Hoyer, for whom I was named, retired from
farming before I was born, and appeared to me as a sedentary
talker, with an ash-colored mustache, high-top buttoned
shoes, and a beautiful stately way of delivering his pronounce-
ments to deaf ears. He should have been a politician, my father always said of "Pop" Hoyer. This was not entirely a
compliment; my father's generation had a Menckenesque
contempt for politicians. My grandfather, on the other hand,
owned a keen country sense of the courthouse as a holy center, pronounced the words "burgess" and "alderman" and
"judge" in a reverential manner, and took that genially reduc-
tive view of human motives that is, after all, the basis of the
American political system. In men like him, ornate arguers
and ironical listeners, the citizens of the rural Republic sought
their spokesmen and discovered their provincial interests.
Through his Democratic prejudices I looked back, unknow-
ingly, into the Jacksonian Democracy—anti-tariff, anti-
Bank—whereby America's yeomen, north and south, took
power from the seaboard aristocrats and bankers. Four decades later, under the stalking horse of abolitionism,[29] these

---

[29]The only political story of my grandfather's that I remember concerned the
hypocrisy of abolitionist Quakers. Here is the story as told by John Hook, in *The
Poorhouse Fair* (1959, pp. 92–3): "The Quakers among the city dwellers had a great
reputation for good works, and in Buchanan's day were much lauded for passing
the runaway slaves on up to Canada. Ah. But the truth of it was, this old fella who
was the patriarch of the sect would harbor the negroes in the summer, when they
would work his fields for nothing, and then when the cold weather came, and the
crops were in, he would turn them out, when they had never known a winter before. One black man balked, you know, and the old fella standing on the doorstep
said so sharp: 'Dost thou not hear thy Master calleth thee?'"

same urban forces, swollen black and mighty, took power back. Like Buchanan, my grandfather depended upon and distrusted women; smoked cigars; obeyed the law; was a Mason; loved cronyship.[30] And as with Buchanan, though he read his Bible to tatters, he lived, I fear, in a world purely human. Will people ever talk about each other so avidly again, or fashion of the lives of those they know such a treasure of polished nuggets and gimcracks of gossip? How telegraphic, how unloving, by comparison, our own gossip is!

Even older than my grandfather was Uncle John Spotts, his sister Hannah's husband. Uncle John, shorter than five feet, with a hook nose and large-lidded eyes in deep sockets, spoke with an antique voice, an old-fashioned super-palatal wheeze that merged with the dark, somehow tropical greenery outside his house and the smells of fresh-baked pie dough and unused plush parlor chairs inside. Though his hand bunched into blue knobs as it gripped the curve of his cane, he was dapper, in starched pinstripe shirt and broad suspenders, and his inner knit, I felt as a child, was as clean and tight as the wickerwork of his porch chairs. Nearly a hundred Pennsylvania summers lived in him, hazy farm summers where only the springhouse was cool. His kindly, eerie wheeze of a voice, sighing "Johnny" with a caressing tone of lament, arose from a green world where men would not breathe again, a Pennsylvania dying about us, though its buildings like bones remained. I wanted to dive into that lost green, and set a novel there.

At some moments of research I touched something live. In the great round reading room of the British Museum, with its aquarium whispering, they brought me a book about Henry

---

[30]"He . . . delighted more than any public man I have known in what is sometimes called 'cronyship.'" —Foote, *Casket of Reminiscences*, p. 113.

Clay published in 1864; its pages had never been cut, I had to slice them with the edge of a credit card. Startled British faces looked around at the tearing sound. I wanted to explain, I was innocent, more than innocent; I was the prince whose kiss this book had been awaiting, asleep, for over a century. Then, at the Historical Society of Pennsylvania, a few floors above the muggy hullaballoo of Philadelphia, I held in my hands the very sheets of paper—eight of them, legal-length—upon which Jeremiah Black, his gorgeous flowing hand intact after a sleepless night and a hectic month, had written out his objections and emendations to Buchanan's proposed reply to the South Carolina "Commissioners." For a moment— December 30, 1860—American history had flowed through these sheets, these arabesques and furious hatchings of ink. A tide had turned that morning. The South's long hold on Washington had been broken; the possibility of a negotiated, peaceful secession had passed. The Union's course had been set, here, in my hands. And again, one winter, unable to make the novel move, unable to strike the music—the chords of de-tail given momentum by significance—that, as Henry James had warned, can only be elicited from "the palpable present *intimate* that throbs responsive,"[31] I impulsively, desperately

---

[31] On October 5, 1901, James wrote to Sarah Orne Jewett apropos of her novel *The Tory Lover*: "The 'historic' novel is, for me, condemned even in cases of labour as delicate as yours, to a fatal *cheapness*, for the simple reason that the difficulty of the job is inordinate and that a mere *escamotage*, in the interest of ease, and of the abysmal public *naiveté* becomes inevitable. You may multiply the little facts that can be got from pictures and documents, relics and prints as much as you like—*the* real thing is almost impossible to do and in its essence the whole effect is as nought: I mean the invention, the representation of the old *consciousness*, the soul, the sense, the horizon, the vision of individuals in whose minds half the things that make ours, that make the modern world were non-existent. You have to think with your modern apparatus a man, a woman—or rather fifty—whose own thinking was in-tensely otherwise conditioned, you have to simplify back by an amazing tour de force—and even then it's all humbug. . . ." —*Selected Letters*, edited by Leon Edel, pp. 202–3.

flew south from Boston, hoping that the sight of Wheatland, in Lancaster, might break the block. The flight to Newark was delayed; I missed the connecting flight and had to drive a rented car through New Jersey, to the Pennsylvania Turnpike. Winter held the woods and wide fields in suspense. I passed the Morgantown exit that so many times had taken me home and drove into Lancaster as dusk was falling. Buchanan's dusty road to Marietta is now a residential street. It rises out of the old downtown, where the courtly street names and colonial brick houses persist amid a modern clutter of commerce and reconstruction; and then Marietta Avenue slightly falls, and on the left, back safe on its great lawn, stands Wheatland. Of orangish brick, the mansion, with its narrow windowless sides and rather sprightly, Frenchified façade, feels intimate—or felt so that day, when snow hushed its grounds, and I was the only visitor. The driveway had been plowed, but the paths were unshovelled. No caretaker moved to intercept me. Solitary as a burglar, as a lover, I waded to the windows and looked in. Through wavery panes rapidly darkening, I glimpsed planes of wallpaper, an oval mirror topped by an eagle, balusters of the stairway in whose newel post is sealed the rolled-up mortgage papers and at whose head rests (I knew) the porcelain bowl given Buchanan by the Mikado of Japan, the largest piece of porcelain in the world, mistakenly sold out of the

---

In his introduction to *The Aspern Papers* in the New York edition (1909), however, James concedes "a palpable imaginable *visitable* past—in the nearer distances and the clearer mysteries, the marks and signs of a world we may reach over to as by making a long arm we grasp an object at the other end of our own table. The table is the one, the common expanse, and where we lean, so stretching, we find it firm and continuous. That, to my imagination, is the past fragrant of all, or of almost all, the poetry of the thing outlived and lost and gone, and yet in which the precious element of closeness, telling so of connexions but tasting so of differences, remains appreciable. With more moves back the element of the appreciable shrinks—just as the charm of looking over a garden-wall into another garden breaks down when successions of walls appear."

White House by Mary Lincoln and many years later recovered for Buchanan's estate. Creeping along the wall, I peered as into James's "garden" into the windows of the library where the old Functionary had spun his web of letters and received job-seekers, power-brokers, cronies, and neighbors. The leather settee, the glass-fronted bookcases, the framed posters and flags, even the basket of pretzels the Lancaster Historical Society has set upon the center table—I could make out all these, but coming closer had put me further away. The furniture of his life remained sealed upon its mystery. The house was closed for the season. I could not get in.

Nor could I get into his life and make my novel there. The plan was to have him dying and in delirium or dream reliving. His days, the correct dates running along in the margin like the ticking of a clock, would flow unchronologically one out of the other, revealing the "veins" of his psychology, of his fate. There were even four chapter titles, alliterative as I like them: *Love, Law, Duty, Death.* But researched details failed to act like remembered ones, they had no palpable medium of the half-remembered in which to swim; my imagination was frozen by the theoretical discoverability of *everything*. An actual man, Buchanan, had done this and this, exactly so, once; and no other way. There was no air. Atoms of the known lit up an abyss of the unknowable. In the end, a play seemed possible. Let the designers of sets and costumes solve the surfaces. Let theatrical unreality equal historical unreality. Let the actors themselves be the "veins." Let speech, which is all impalpable that remains to us of the dead, be all. Some scenes, like that of the Colemans' party, I took from the aborted novel; other scenes, like his walk with Jackson and the Cabinet struggles, had only to be synthesized from existing accounts. The pages did at last accumulate. In the course of their accumulation, I broke my leg, turned forty, buried my father. So be it. *Sufficient to the day is the evil thereof.* Here is Buchanan, I am rid of him, and this book, a mosaic with more tesserae than matrix, constitutes, I trust, my final volume of homage to my native state, whose mild misty doughy middleness, between immoderate norths and souths, remains for me, being my first taste of life, the authentic taste.

## Last Words

"O Lord, God Almighty, as Thou wilt!" were Buchanan's actual last words, attested to in Nevin's funeral sermon, though who heard them is not given; Nevin describes them as "whispered in the ear of anxious affection bending over him, as he was turned somewhat painfully upon his bed." The words "All that is heavy is fallen away" I took from a letter written by Alfred Schmidt-Sas, a teacher and musician executed by the Nazis in April 1943. Schmidt-Sas had been expecting his execution from hour to hour for months; on April 4, 1943, he wrote [his wife?]:

> . . . in another five hours I shall be executed. A great peace fills me, and a feeling of great lightness. All that is heavy is fallen away. And never have I possessed your love and the love of the others so purely, so deeply, and so unflawed. I am happy in an inexplicable fashion. Keep me thus in memory. . . .

He was not executed until five days later, and lived to write another letter, and, with manacled hands, a poem beginning and ending, "O strangely luminous life so close to death." Printed in a book of last messages from German (mostly practicing Christian) resisters to Nazism entitled *Dying We*

*Live* (edited by Helmut Gollwitzer, Käthe Kuhn, Reinhold Schneider; translated by Reinhard C. Kuhn; published by Pantheon in 1956; pp. 177–9).

## Posthumous

Letters in the Library of Congress show that Buchanan's two principal survivors, his niece Harriet Lane Johnston and his brother Edward Buchanan, fell to squabbling over who was going to write the dead man's biography. Joseph B. Baker, whom Buchanan had appointed Collector to the Port of Philadelphia, found himself in the middle. On August 4, 1870, he wrote Harriet that Rev. Mr. Buchanan had turned down some proposal from the Johnstons about the selection and payment of the biographer: he quoted Edward Buchanan's letter: "I cannot consent even to consider any proposition from them, looking to a co-partnership with them in anything." Baker, finding it "very trying to me to write anything that may cause further irritations," proposed that the Johnstons allow the statesman's younger brother "to proceed in his own way in the business—not only the Ex-President's kinsmen but the public will find him responsible for the manner in which the work is executed."

Harriet drafted a scorching reply to Baker, in a style not found in her letters when "Nunc" was alive to moderate her heat, but that shows that in at least one woman's heart the old bachelor left a legacy of loyal passion:

My dear Mr Baker—

I am not surprised at Mr E Y Buchanans sentiments as expressed in his letter to you—for where a man has done another a very gross wrong he can never forgive him. Clergymen are no exceptions to this rule. Mr F. Y B made a mistake in imagining we desired a "co-partnership" with him in anything. We have tried that, & find that he cannot stand by it even when the letters of agreement are *signed*, sealed & delivered. He is only trying to dodge the necessity of giving his money, but he shall be shamed into it at last. Knowing Mr E Y Buchanan as I do you cannot ask me to allow him "to proceed in his own way in the business of the Biography." You think "the Public, & the Ex Presidents kinsmen," will hold *him* responsible for the work. Why, my dear Sir, "the public" do not even know of the existence of Mr Buchanan & his kinsmen are too well acquainted with his want of wisdom, energy, decision, judgment, sentiment & feeling to think of *him* as the responsible person about the Biography. I cannot consent to leaving anything to him in which my dear Uncle's fame is concerned. *That* is *too dear to me*.

JOHN UPDIKE was born in Shillington, Pennsylvania, in 1932. He graduated from Harvard College in 1954 and spent a year in Oxford, England, at the Ruskin School of Drawing and Fine Art. From 1955 to 1957 he was a member of the staff of *The New Yorker.* His novels have won the Pulitzer Prize, the National Book Award, the National Book Critics Circle Award, the Rosenthal Foundation Award, and the William Dean Howells Medal. In 2007 he received the Gold Medal for Fiction from the American Academy of Arts and Letters. John Updike died in January 2009.